FILIBUSTERS, CLOTURE AND HOLDS IN THE SENATE

LAWS AND LEGISLATION

Additional books in this series can be found on Nova's website under the Series tab.

Additional E-books in this series can be found on Nova's website under the E-books tab.

LAWS AND LEGISLATION

FILIBUSTERS, CLOTURE AND HOLDS IN THE SENATE

DAVID J. GILGRAM
EDITOR

Nova Science Publishers, Inc.
New York

LIBRARY OF CONGRESS CATALOGING-IN-PUBLICATION DATA

Filibusters, cloture and holds in the Senate / editors David J. Gilgram.

p. cm.

Includes index.

Consists of reports prepared by the Congressional Research Service.

ISBN 978-1-61728-925-5 (softcover)

1. United States. Congress. Senate--Rules and practice. 2. United States. Congress. Senate--Cloture. 3. Filibusters (Political science)--United States. I. Gilgram, David J. II. Library of Congress. Congressional Research Service.

KF4984.F55 2010

328.73'0775--dc22-2010025933

Published by Nova Science Publishers, Inc. ✦ *New York*

CONTENTS

PREFACE

Filibustering includes any use of dilatory or obstructive tactics to block a measure by preventing it from coming to a vote. The possibility of filibusters exists because Senate rules place few limits on Senator's rights and opportunities in the legislative process. Senate Rule XXII, however, known as the "cloture rule," enables Senators to end a filibuster on any debatable matter the Senate is considering. Sixteen Senators initiate this process by presenting a motion to end the debate. Consequently, "holds" are an informal device unique to the upper body. They permit a single Senator or any number of Senators to stop, temporarily or permanently, floor consideration of measures or matters that are available to be scheduled by the Senate. This book discusses major aspects of Senate procedure related to filibusters, cloture and holds.

Chapter 1 - The filibuster is widely viewed as one of the Senate's most characteristic procedural features. Filibustering includes any use of dilatory or obstructive tactics to block a measure by preventing it from coming to a vote. The possibility of filibusters exists because Senate rules place few limits on Senators' rights and opportunities in the legislative process.

In particular, a Senator who seeks recognition usually has a right to the floor if no other Senator is speaking, and then may speak for as long as he or she wishes. Also, there is no motion by which a simple majority of the Senate can stop a debate and allow the Senate to vote in favor of an amendment, a bill or resolution, or any other debatable question. Almost every bill, indeed, is potentially subject to two filibusters before the Senate votes on whether to pass it: first, a filibuster on a motion to proceed to the bill's consideration; and second, after the Senate agrees to this motion, a filibuster on the bill itself.

Senate Rule XXII, however, known as the "cloture rule," enables Senators to end a filibuster on any debatable matter the Senate is considering. Sixteen

Senators initiate this process by presenting a motion to end the debate. The Senate does not vote on this cloture motion until the second day of session after the motion is made. Then, for most matters, it requires the votes of at least three-fifths of all Senators (normally 60 votes) to invoke cloture. (Invoking cloture on a proposal to amend the Senate's standing rules requires the support of two-thirds of the Senators present and voting.)

The primary effect of invoking cloture on a question is to impose a maximum of 30 additional hours for considering that question. This 30-hour period for consideration encompasses all time consumed by roll call votes, quorum calls, and other actions, as well as the time used for debate. During this 30-hour period, in general, no Senator may speak for more than one hour (although several Senators can have additional time yielded to them). Under cloture, as well, the only amendments that Senators can offer are amendments that are germane and that were submitted in writing before the cloture vote took place. Finally, the presiding officer also enjoys certain additional powers under cloture: for example, to count to determine whether a quorum is present, and to rule amendments, motions, and other actions out of order on the grounds that they are dilatory.

Chapter 2 - Cloture is the only means by which the Senate can vote to limit debate on a matter, and thereby overcome a possible filibuster. It would be erroneous, however, to assume that cases in which cloture is sought are the same as those in which a filibuster occurs. Cloture may be sought when no filibuster is taking place, and filibusters may occur without cloture being sought.

Until 1949, cloture could not be invoked on nominations, and before 1980 this action was attempted only twice. From the 96th Congress (1979-1980) through the 102nd (199 1-1992), cloture was never sought on more than three nominations in a single Congress, but since then this level has been exceeded four times.

From 1949 through 2008, cloture was sought on 68 nominations, and invoked on 31. The Senate voted to reject cloture on 20 of the remaining 37 nominations, and on the final 17 nominations no cloture motion received a vote. Seventeen of the 68 nominees failed of confirmation, and 11 of these 17 were considered during the 108th Congress (2003-2004). In the 103rd Congress (1993- 1994) and the 109th Congress (2005-2006) most of the cloture attempts were to executive branch nominations, but in all other Congresses nominations to the federal bench predominated.

Cloture has been sought on four nominations to the Supreme Court. In 1968, a cloture vote on the motion to proceed to consider the nomination of

Abe Fortas to be Chief Justice failed. In 1971, when he was first appointed to the court, and again in 1986 when he was nominated to be Chief Justice, opponents of William H. Rehnquist mounted a filibuster. Though the cloture vote in 1971 was unsuccessful, Rehnquist was confirmed to the court; in 1986, the cloture vote was successful. In 2006, the Senate successfully invoked cloture on the nomination of Samuel A. Alito, Jr., to be an associate justice on the Supreme Court.

Chapter 3 - Long known for its emphasis on lengthy deliberation, the Senate in most circumstances allows its Members to debate issues for as long as they want. Further, the Senate has few ways either to limit the duration of debates or to bring filibusters (extended "talkathons") to an end. For instance, a Senator may offer a non-debatable motion to table (or kill) an amendment or he or she might ask unanimous consent to restrict debate on pending matters. The Senate has one formal rule — Rule XXII — for imposing limits on the further consideration of an issue. Called the cloture rule (for closure of debate), Rule XXII became part of the Senate's rulebook in 1917 and has been amended several times since.

Under its current formulation, Rule XXII requires a cloture petition (signed by 16 Senators) to be presented to the Senate. Two days later, and one hour after the Senate convenes, the presiding officer is required to order a live quorum call (often waived by unanimous consent) and, after its completion, to put this question to the membership: "Is it the sense of the Senate that debate shall be brought to a close?" If three-fifths of the entire Senate membership (60 of 100) votes in the affirmative, cloture is invoked and the Senate is subject to post-cloture procedures that will eventually end the debate and bring the clotured question (a bill, amendment, or motion, for example) to a vote. (To end debate on a measure or motion to amend Senate rules requires approval by two-thirds of the Senators present and voting.)

If cloture is invoked under the terms of Rule XXII, then Senate floor activity is thereafter subject to a variety of conditions and constraints. Several of the main post- cloture features include:

Chapter 4 - *Holds* are an informal device unique to the upper body. They permit a single Senator or any number of Senators to stop—sometimes temporarily, sometimes permanently—floor consideration of measures or matters that are available to be scheduled by the Senate. A hold, in brief, is a request by a Senator to his or her party leader to delay floor action on a measure or matter. It is up to the majority leader to decide whether, or for how long, he will honor a colleague's hold. Scheduling the business of the Senate is the fundamental prerogative of the majority leader, and it is done in consultation with the minority leader.

Chapter 5 - When the Honest Leadership and Open Government Act (S. 1, 110th Congress) was signed into law on September 14, 2007, Section 512 of that statute specifically addressed the issue of secret "holds." Holds are a longstanding custom of the Senate that enabled Members to provide notice to their party leader of their intent to object on the floor to taking up or passing a measure or matter. Their potency as a blocking, delaying, or bargaining device is linked to Senators' ability to conduct filibusters or object to unanimous consent agreements or requests. The new holds process outlined in Section 512 is designed to constrain the frequency of anonymous holds and promote more openness and transparency with respect to their use. Ultimately, it is up to the majority leader of the Senate—who sets the chamber's agenda after consulting various people—to decide whether, or for how long, he will honor a colleague's hold.

In: Filibusters, Cloture and Holds in the Senate   ISBN: 978-1-61728-925-5
Editors: David J. Gilgram   © 2010 Nova Science Publishers, Inc.

Chapter 1

FILIBUSTERS AND CLOTURE IN THE SENATE*

Richard S. Beth, Valerie Heitshusen and Betsy Palmer

SUMMARY

The filibuster is widely viewed as one of the Senate's most characteristic procedural features. Filibustering includes any use of dilatory or obstructive tactics to block a measure by preventing it from coming to a vote. The possibility of filibusters exists because Senate rules place few limits on Senators' rights and opportunities in the legislative process.

In particular, a Senator who seeks recognition usually has a right to the floor if no other Senator is speaking, and then may speak for as long as he or she wishes. Also, there is no motion by which a simple majority of the Senate can stop a debate and allow the Senate to vote in favor of an amendment, a bill or resolution, or any other debatable question. Almost every bill, indeed, is potentially subject to two filibusters before the Senate votes on whether to pass it: first, a filibuster on a motion to proceed to the bill's consideration; and second, after the Senate agrees to this motion, a filibuster on the bill itself.

Senate Rule XXII, however, known as the "cloture rule," enables Senators to end a filibuster on any debatable matter the Senate is considering. Sixteen Senators initiate this process by presenting a motion to end the debate. The

---

* This is an edited, reformatted and augmented version of a CRS Report for Congress publication dated March 2010.

Senate does not vote on this cloture motion until the second day of session after the motion is made. Then, for most matters, it requires the votes of at least three-fifths of all Senators (normally 60 votes) to invoke cloture. (Invoking cloture on a proposal to amend the Senate's standing rules requires the support of two-thirds of the Senators present and voting.)

The primary effect of invoking cloture on a question is to impose a maximum of 30 additional hours for considering that question. This 30-hour period for consideration encompasses all time consumed by roll call votes, quorum calls, and other actions, as well as the time used for debate. During this 30-hour period, in general, no Senator may speak for more than one hour (although several Senators can have additional time yielded to them). Under cloture, as well, the only amendments that Senators can offer are amendments that are germane and that were submitted in writing before the cloture vote took place. Finally, the presiding officer also enjoys certain additional powers under cloture: for example, to count to determine whether a quorum is present, and to rule amendments, motions, and other actions out of order on the grounds that they are dilatory.

The ability of Senators to engage in filibusters has a profound and pervasive effect on how the Senate conducts its business on the floor. In the face of a threatened filibuster, for example, the majority leader may decide not to call a bill up for floor consideration, or to defer calling it up if there are other, equally important bills that the Senate can consider and pass without undue delay. Similarly, the prospect of a filibuster can persuade a bill's proponents to accept changes in the bill that they do not support, but that are necessary to prevent an actual filibuster.

The filibuster is widely viewed as one of the Senate's most distinctive procedural features. Today, the term is most often used to refer to Senators holding the floor in extended debate. More generally, however, "filibustering" includes any tactics aimed at blocking a measure by preventing it from coming to a vote.

As a consequence, the Senate has no specific "rules for filibustering." Instead, possibilities for filibustering exist because Senate Rules deliberately *lack* provisions that would place specific limits on Senators' rights and opportunities in the legislative process. In particular, those Rules establish no generally applicable limits on the length of debate, nor any motions by which a majority could vote to bring a debate to an end, or even limit it.

The only Senate Rule that permits the body, by vote, to bring consideration of a matter to an end is paragraph 2 of Rule XXII, known as the "cloture rule." Invoking cloture requires a super- majority vote (usually 60 out of 100 Senators), and doing so does not terminate consideration, but only imposes a time limit. Cloture also imposes restrictions on certain other potentially dilatory procedures. In recent years, as a result, cloture has increasingly been used to overcome filibusters being conducted not only by debate, but through various other delaying tactics.

This chapter discusses major aspects of Senate procedure related to filibusters and cloture. The two, however, are not always as closely linked in practice as they are in popular conception. Even when opponents of a measure resort to extended debate or other tactics of delay, supporters may not decide to seek cloture (although this situation seems to have been more common in earlier decades than today). In recent times, conversely, Senate leadership has increasingly made use of cloture as a normal tool for managing the flow of business on the floor, even at times when no evident filibuster has yet occurred.

These considerations imply that the presence or absence of cloture attempts cannot be taken as a reliable guide to the presence or absence of filibusters. Inasmuch as filibustering does not depend on the use of any specific rules, whether a filibuster is present is always a matter of judgment. It is also a matter of degree; filibusters may be conducted with greater or lesser determination and persistence. For all these reasons, it is not feasible to construct a definitive list of filibusters.

The following discussion focuses chiefly on the conduct of filibusters through extended debate, and on cloture as a means of overcoming them. The discussion does not encompass all possible contingencies or consider every relevant precedent. Authoritative information on cloture procedure can be found under that heading in *Riddick's Senate Procedure*.[1] Senators and staff also may wish to consult the Senate Parliamentarian on any question concerning the Senate's procedural rules, precedents, and practices.

THE RIGHT TO DEBATE

The core rule of the Senate governing floor debate is paragraph 1(a) of Rule XIX, which states that:

> When a Senator desires to speak, he shall rise and address the Presiding Officer, and shall not proceed until he is recognized, and the Presiding Officer shall recognize the Senator who shall first address him. No Senator shall interrupt another Senator in debate without his consent, and to obtain

such consent he shall first address the Presiding Officer, and no Senator shall speak more than twice upon any one question in debate on the same legislative day without leave of the Senate, which shall be determined without debate.

This is essentially all that the Senate's rules have to say about the right to speak on the floor, so the rule is just as important for what it *does not* say as for what it *does* say. The lack of discretion by the chair in recognizing Senators, and the lack of time limits on debate, combine to create the possibility of filibusters by debate.

The Right to Recognition

Rule XIX affords the presiding officer no choice and no discretion in recognition. As a general rule, if a Senator seeks recognition when no other Senator has the floor, the presiding officer must recognize him or her. The presiding officer may not decline to recognize the Senator, whether for reasons of personal preference or partisan advantage, or to enable the Senate to reach a vote on the pending matter. As a result, when the Senate is considering any debatable question, it cannot vote on the question so long as any Senator wants to be recognized to debate it.

If more than one Senator seeks recognition, Rule XIX directs the presiding officer to recognize whichever is the first to do so. The result is that, although no Senator can be sure that he or she will be recognized *promptly* for debate on a pending question, each can be sure of recognition *eventually*. As Senate rules provide for no motions that could have the effect of terminating debate, a Senator can do nothing while she or he has the floor that would preclude another Senator from being recognized afterwards. (The motion to table and time agreements by unanimous consent, both of which represent partial exceptions to this statement, are discussed later).

By well-established precedent and practice, the Senate does not comply strictly with the requirement that the first Senator addressing the chair be recognized. All Senators accept that the majority leader and then the minority leader must be able to secure recognition if they are to do some of the things the Senate expects them to do: to arrange the daily agenda and weekly schedule, and to make motions and propound unanimous consent agreements necessary for the relatively orderly conduct of business on the floor. In practice, the party leaders receive preference in recognition. This means that, if two Senators are seeking recognition at more or less the same time, and one of them is a party floor leader, the presiding officer recognizes the leader (and the majority leader in preference to the minority leader). Next after these two leaders, the majority and minority floor managers of legislation being debated also generally are accorded preference in recognition. They receive this preference because they also bear responsibilities for ensuring an orderly process of considering a measure.

The Right to Speak at Length and the Two-Speech Rule

Under Rule XIX, unless any special limits on debate are in effect, Senators who have been recognized may speak for as long as they wish.[2] They usually cannot be forced to cede the floor, or even interrupted, without their consent. (There are some exceptions: for example, Senators can lose the floor if they violate the Senate's standards of decorum in debate, or, as discussed later, they may be interrupted for the presentation of a cloture motion.)

Rule XIX places no limit on the length of individual speeches or on the number of Senators who may speak on a pending question. It does, however, tend to limit the possibility of extended debate by its provision that "no Senator shall speak more than twice upon any one question in debate on the same legislative day without leave of the Senate, which shall be determined without debate." This provision, commonly called the "two-speech rule," limits each Senator to making two speeches per day, however long each speech may be, on each debatable question that the Senate considers. A Senator who has made two speeches on a single question becomes ineligible to be recognized for another speech on the same question on the same day.

The "day" during which a Senator can make no more than two speeches on the same question is not a calendar day, but a legislative day. A legislative day ends only with an adjournment, so that, whenever the Senate recesses overnight, rather than adjourning, the same legislative day continues into the next calendar day. A legislative day may therefore extend over several calendar days. The leadership may continue to recess the Senate, rather than adjourning, as a means of attempting to overcome a filibuster by compelling filibustering Senators to exhaust their opportunities of gaining recognition.

Senators rarely invoke the two-speech rule. Sometimes, however, they may insist that the two- speech rule be enforced, as a means of attempting to overcome a filibuster. On such occasions, nevertheless, Senators often can circumvent the two-speech rule by making a motion or offering an amendment that constitutes a new and different debatable question. For example, each Senator can make two speeches on each bill, each first-degree amendment to a bill, and each second- degree amendment to each of those amendments as well.

In recent practice, the Senate considers that being recognized and engaging in debate constitutes a speech. The Senate, however, does not consider "that recognition for any purpose [constitutes] a speech." Currently effective precedents have held that "certain procedural motions and requests were examples of actions that did not constitute speeches for purposes of the two speech rule." These matters include such things as making a parliamentary inquiry and suggesting the absence of a quorum.[3] Nevertheless, if a Senator is recognized for a substantive comment, however brief, on the pending question, that remark may count as a speech.

The Motion to Table

There is one way in which the Senate can end debate on a question even though there may be Senators who still might want to speak on it. During the debate, it is normally possible for a Senator to move to table the pending question (more formally, to lay the question on the table). The motion is not debatable, and requires only a simple majority vote to be adopted. In the Senate, to table something is to kill it. So when the Senate votes to table a matter, it therebydisposes of the matter permanently and adversely. The Senate frequently disposes of amendments by voting to table them, rather than by taking what often are called "up or down" votes to agree to (or not agree to) the amendment itself.

If there is a unanimous consent agreement in effect that limits the time for debate, the motion to table may not be offered until the time is consumed. Also, in order to offer the motion, a Senator must first be recognized; another Senator who has already been recognized may not be interrupted for a motion to table, no matter how long he or she has been speaking. Within these limitations, if a majority of Senators oppose a matter, the motion to table may enable them to prevail at a time of their choosing. By this means, Senators can prevent a debate from continuing indefinitely, if they are prepared to reject the amendment, motion, or bill that is being debated. (If, on the other hand, opponents of a matter do not command enough support to table it, they may decide to extend the debate by conducting what supporters of the matter might well characterize as a filibuster.)

The motion to table, however, offers no means for supporters of a matter to overcome a filibuster being conducted against it through extended debate. If the Senate agrees to a motion to table, the debate is brought to an end, but only at the cost of defeating the matter. If the Senate votes against the tabling motion, the matter remains before the Senate, and Senators can resume debating it at length.

Instead, for purposes of overcoming filibusters, the chief use of the motion to table arises when the filibuster is being conducted through the offering of potentially dilatory amendments and motions. For example, supporters of a filibuster may offer amendments in order to renew their right to recognition under the two-speech rule. Each time the Senate tables such an amendment, it can continue debate on the underlying bill, or at least can go on to consider other amendments.

THE CONDUCT OF FILIBUSTERS

Conducting a filibuster by extended debate is simple, though it can be physically demanding. A Senator seeks recognition and, once recognized, speaks at length. When that first Senator concludes and yields the floor, another Senator seeks recognition and continues the debate. The debate can proceed in this way until all the participating Senators have made their two speeches on the pending question. Then it usually is possible to offer an amendment, or make some other motion, in order to create a new debatable question, on which the same Senators can make two more speeches.

There is no need for the participating Senators to monopolize the debate. What is important is that someone speak, not that it be someone on their side of the question. Although one purpose of a filibuster is to try to change the minds of Senators who support the question being debated, the purpose of delay is served by Senators speaking, no matter which side of the question they take.

Germaneness of Debate

More often than not, there is no need for the debate to be germane to the question being considered, with one important exception. Paragraph 1(b) of Rule XIX (often called the "Pastore rule" in recognition of former Senator John Pastore of Rhode Island) requires that debate be germane each calendar day during the first three hours after the Senate begins to consider itsunfinished or pending legislative business. In other words, the time consumed by the majority and minority leaders, and any speeches during "routine morning business," at the beginning of a daily session is not included in this three-hour period. The Senate can waive this germaneness requirement by unanimous consent or by agreeing to a non-debatable motion for that purpose.

Like the two-speech rule, the Pastore rule usually is not enforced. During filibusters, however, Senators may be called upon to comply with the germaneness requirement on debate when it is in effect. In practice, this does not put much extra burden on participating Senators, because most speeches made during filibusters today tend to be germane anyway.

In earlier times, filibustering Senators were known to speak about virtually anything. In his 1940 study of filibusters, Franklin Burdette reported that Senator Huey Long of Louisiana—

> would dictate for the benefit of the *Congressional Record* recipes for cooking upon which his authoritative advice had been regularly in demand in Washington social circles .... He then proceeded to tell the Senate at great length and in meticulous detail how to fry oysters. Nor did he omit a rambling discourse on the subject of 'potlikker.'[4]

At that time, the Senate had no rule of germaneness in debate, even during the first three hours of each day, but even at the time to which Burdette referred, a discourse such as Senator Long's was unusual.

Yielding the Floor and Yielding for Questions

A Senator who has the floor for purposes of debate must remain standing and must speak more or less continuously.[5] Complying with these requirements obviously becomes more of a strain as time passes. However, Senators must be careful when they try to give some relief to their colleagues who are speaking. Senate precedents prohibit Senators from yielding the floor to each other. To gain the floor, a Senator must seek recognition from the presiding officer. Thus, if a Senator simply yields to a colleague, he or she has yielded (relinquished) the floor, however inadvertently. This is another one of those Senate procedures that often is not observed during the normal conduct of business on the floor. But during a filibuster involving extended floor debate, Senators are much more likely to insist on it being observed.

A Senator may yield to a colleague without losing the floor only if the Senator yields for a question.[6] With this in mind, a colleague of a filibustering Senator may give that Senator some relief by asking him or her to yield for a question. The Senator who retains control of the floor must remain standing while the question is being asked. The peculiar advantage of this tactic is that it sometimes takes Senators quite some time to ask their question, and the presiding officer is reluctant to force them to state their question before they are ready to do so. In this way, participating Senators can extend the debate through an exchange of what sometimes are long questions followed by short answers, rather than by relying exclusively on a series of long, uninterrupted speeches.

Quorums and Quorum Calls

There are ways other than debate by which Senators can delay and sometimes even prevent the Senate from voting on a question that it is considering. For example, each amendment that is offered on the Senate floor must be read in full before debate on it can begin, although the Senate usually agrees by unanimous consent to waive the reading. In addition, quorum calls can be demanded not for the purpose of confirming or securing the presence of a quorum, but in order to consume time.

A Senator who has been recognized can "suggest the absence of a quorum," asking in effect whether the Senate is complying with the constitutional requirement that a quorum—a majority of all Senators—be present for the Senate to conduct business. The presiding officer normally does not have the authority to count to determine whether a quorum actually is present (which is rarely the case), and so directs the clerk to call the roll.

Senators usually use quorum calls to suspend the Senate's floor proceedings temporarily, perhaps to discuss a procedural or policy problem or to await the arrival of a certain Senator. In those cases, the clerk calls the roll very slowly and, before the call of the roll is completed, the Senate agrees by unanimous consent to call off the quorum call (to "dispense with further proceedings under the quorum call"). Because the absence of a quorum has not actually been demonstrated, the Senate can resume its business. Such quorum calls can be time-consuming and so can serve the interests of filibustering Senators.

During a filibuster, however, the clerk may be directed by the leadership to call the roll more rapidly, as if a roll call vote were in progress. Doing so reduces the time that the quorum call consumes, but it also creates the real possibility that the quorum call may demonstrate that a quorum in fact is not present. In that case, the Senate has only two options: to adjourn, or to take steps necessary to secure the presence of enough absent Senators to create a quorum. Typically, the majority leader or the majority floor manager opts for the latter course, and makes a motion that the sergeant at arms secure the attendance of absent Senators, and then asks for a roll call vote on that motion. Senators who did not respond to the quorum call are likely to come to the floor for the roll call vote on this motion. Almost always, therefore, the vote establishes that a quorum is present, so the Senate can resume its business without the sergeant at arms actually having to execute the Senate's directive.

This process also can be time-consuming because of the time required to conduct the roll call vote just discussed. Nonetheless, the proponents of the bill (or other matter) being filibustered may prefer that the roll be called quickly because it requires unanimous consent to call off a routine quorum call, in which the clerk calls the roll very slowly, before it is completed. A filibustering Senator has only to suggest the absence of a quorum and then object to calling off the quorum call in order to provoke a motion to secure the attendance of absentees and (with the support of at least 10 other Senators) a roll call vote on that motion. If this motion is likely to be necessary, one way or the other, it is usually in the interests of the bill's proponents to have the motion made(and agreed to) as soon as possible.

When Senators suggest the absence of a quorum, however, they lose the floor. Also, "[i]t is not in order for a Senator to demand a quorum call if no business has intervened since the last call; business must intervene before a second quorum call or between calls if the question is raised or apoint of order made."[7] These restrictions limit the extent to which quorum calls may be used as means of conducting filibusters.

Roll Call Voting

As the preceding discussion indicates, roll call votes are another source of delay. Any question put to the Senate for its decision requires a vote, and a minimum of 11 Senators can require that it be a roll call vote. Each such vote consumes at least 15 minutes unless the Senate agrees in advance to reduce the time for voting.[8]

The Constitution provides that the "yeas and nays" shall be ordered "at the desire of one-fifth of those present" (Article I, Section 5). Because a quorum is presumed to be present, the Senate requires at least 11 Senators (one-fifth of the minimal quorum of 51) to request a roll call vote on the pending question.

When a Senator wants a roll call vote, other Senators frequently support the request as a courtesy to a colleague. During a filibuster, however, the supporters of the bill or amendment sometimes try to discourage other Senators from supporting requests for time-consuming roll call votes. Also, the proponents sometimes can make it more difficult for their opponents to secure a roll call vote. When the request for a roll call vote is made immediately after a quorum call or another roll call vote, Senators can insist that the request be supported by one-fifth of however many Senators answered that call or cast their votes.[9] Since this is almost certainly more than 51 and, in practice, is much closer to 100, the number of Senators required to secure a roll call can increase to a maximum of 20.

The time allowed for Senators to cast roll call votes is a minimum of 15 minutes, unless the Senate agrees, before the vote begins, to a reduced time. When the 15 minutes expire, the vote usually is left open for some additional time in order to accommodate other Senators who are thought to be en route to the floor to vote. Thus, the actual time for a roll call vote can extend to 20 minutes or more. During filibusters, however, a call for the regular order can lead the presiding officer to announce the result of a roll call vote soon after the 15 minutes allotted for it.

Senators usually can secure two votes in connection with the disposition of each bill, amendment, motion, or other question. The first is the vote on the question itself or on a motion to table it. The second is the vote on a motion to *reconsider* the vote by which the first question was decided (or on a motion to table the motion to reconsider). With sufficient support, roll call votes can be ordered on each *motion. so* that completing action on both of them consumes at least 30 minutes.

Scheduling Filibusters

The leadership typically attempts to arrange the daily schedule of the Senate so that filibusters are not unduly disruptive or inconvenient to Senators. One way to make conducting a filibuster more costly and difficult is to keep the Senate in session until late at night, or even all night, requiring the participating Senators to speak or otherwise consume the Senate's time. During some contentious filibusters of the 1950s, cots were brought into the Senate's anterooms for Senators to use during around-the-clock sessions.

Today, all-night sessions are very unusual. The Senate may not even convene earlier or remain in session later when a filibuster is in progress than it does on other days. One reason may be that filibusters are not the extraordinary and unusual occurrences that they once were. Another may be that Senators are less willing to endure the inconvenience and discomfort of prolonged sessions. Also, leadership may react to a threat of a filibuster by keeping the measure or matter from the floor, at least for a while.

The point about longer, later sessions is important because late-night or all-night sessions put as much or more of a burden on the proponents of the question being debated than on its opponents. The Senators participating in the filibuster need only ensure that at least one of their number always is present on the floor to speak. The proponents of the question, however, need to ensure that a majority of the Senate is present or at least available to respond to a quorum call or roll call vote. If, late in the evening or in the middle of the night, a Senator suggests the absence of a quorum and a quorum does not appear, the Senate must adjourn or at least suspend its proceedings until a quorum is established. This works to the advantage of the filibustering Senators, so the burden rests on their opponents to ensure that the constitutional quorum requirement always can be met.

INVOKING CLOTURE

The procedures for invoking cloture are governed by paragraph 2 of Rule XXII (which also governs procedures under cloture, as discussed later in this chapter).

The process begins when a Senator presents a cloture motion that is signed by 16 Senators, proposing "to bring to a close the debate upon [the pending question]." The motion is presented to the Senate while it is in session, and must be presented while the question on which cloture is sought is pending. For example, it is not in order for a Senator to present a motion to invoke cloture on a bill that the Senate has not yet agreed to consider, or on an amendment that has not yet been offered. A Senator does not need to be recognized by the chair in order to present a cloture petition. The Senator who has the floor may be interrupted for the purpose, but retains the floor thereafter and may continue speaking.

The motion is read to the Senate, but the Senate then returns to whatever business it had been transacting. The Senate does not act on the cloture motion in any way on the day on which it is submitted, or on the following day. Instead, the next action on the motion occurs "on the following calendar day but one"—that is, on the second day of session after it is presented. So if the motion is presented on a Monday, the Senate acts on it on Wednesday.

During the intervening time, the Senate does not have to continue debating the question on which cloture has been proposed, but can turn to other business. One hour after the Senate convenes onthe day the cloture motion has "ripened" or "matured," the presiding officer interrupts the proceedings of the Senate, regardless of what is under consideration at the time, and presents the cloture motion to the Senate for a vote.[10]

At this point the presiding officer is required to direct that an actual (or "live") quorum call take place. (The Senate often waives this quorum call by unanimous consent.) When the presence of a quorum is established, the Senate proceeds, without debate, to vote on the cloture motion: "the Presiding Officer shall, without debate, submit to the Senate by a yea-and-nay vote the question: 'Is it the sense of the Senate that the debate shall be brought to a close?'"[11] The terms of the rule require an automatic roll call vote.

Invoking cloture usually requires a three-fifths vote of the entire Senate— "three-fifths of the Senators duly chosen and sworn." If there are no vacancies, therefore, 60 Senators must vote to invoke cloture. In contrast, most other votes require only a simple majority (that is, 51%) of the Senators present and voting, assuming that those Senators constitute a quorum. In the case of a cloture vote, the key is the number of Senators voting for cloture, not the number voting against. Failing to vote on a cloture motion has the same effect as voting against the motion: it deprives the motion of one of the 60 votes needed to agree to it.

There is an important exception to the three-fifths requirement to invoke cloture. Under Rule XXII, an affirmative vote of two-thirds of the Senators present and voting is required to invoke cloture on a measure or motion to amend the Senate rules. This exception has its origin in the history of the cloture rule. Before 1975, two-thirds of the Senators present and voting (a quorum being present) was required for cloture on all matters. In early 1975, at the beginning of the 94th Congress, Senators sought to amend the rule to make it somewhat easier to invoke cloture. However, some Senators feared that if this effort succeeded, that would only make it easier to amend the rule again, making cloture still easier to invoke. As a compromise, the Senate agreed to move from two-thirds of the Senators present and voting (a maximum of 67 votes) to three-fifths of the Senators duly chosen and sworn (normally, and at a maximum, 60 votes) on all matters except future rules changes, including changes in the cloture rule itself. [12]

If the Senate does vote to invoke cloture, that vote may not be reconsidered. On the other hand, it is in order to reconsider the vote by which the Senate voted against invoking cloture. In current practice, supporters of cloture sometimes enter a motion to reconsider a vote against cloture, so that a second vote on cloture can later occur without a second petition being filed. They can arrange for the second vote to take place at any point when they call up the motion to reconsider, as long as the Senate at that points approved the motion to reconsider. If a simple voting majority agrees to the motion to reconsider, the new vote on the cloture motion then occurs immediately, and cloture is invoked if three-fifths of the full Senate now vote for it.

The Senate sometimes agrees by unanimous consent to alter the way in which various requirements of the cloture rule apply to consideration of a specified matter. In particular, Senators by unanimous consent sometimes permit a cloture motion to be filed on a matter that is not then pending. Also, as mentioned, the required quorum call preceding a cloture vote is oftenwaived by consent. In addition, the Senate may give unanimous consent to adjust the time when the cloture vote will take place. On some occasions, the Senate has even agreed, by unanimous consent, to vote on cloture at a specified time even though no cloture motion is formally filed.

Matters on Which Cloture May be Invoked

Any debatable question that the Senate considers can be filibustered and, therefore, may be the subject of a cloture motion, unless the time for debate is limited by the Senate's rules, by law, or by a unanimous consent agreement. Consequently, Senators may present cloture motions to end debate on bills, resolutions, amendments, conference reports, motions to concur in or amend amendments of the House, executive business (nominations and treaties), and various other debatable motions.

In relation to the Senate's initial consideration of a bill or resolution, there usually can be at least two filibusters: first, a filibuster on the motion to proceed to the measure's consideration; and second, after the Senate agrees to this motion, a filibuster on the measure itself. If the Senate cannot agree to take up a measure by unanimous consent, the majority leader's recourse is to make a motion that the Senate proceed to its consideration. This *motion to proceed*, as it is called, usually is debatable and, consequently, subject to a filibuster.[13] Therefore, the Senate may have to invoke cloture on this motion before being able to vote on it. Once the Senate adopts the motion to proceed and begins consideration of the measure itself, a filibuster on the measure then may begin, so that cloture must be sought anew on the measure itself. Except by unanimous consent, cloture cannot be sought on the measure during consideration of the motion to proceed, because cloture may be moved only on a question that is pending before the Senate. Threatened filibusters on motions to proceed once were rare, but have become more common in recent years.

Threatened filibusters on motions to proceed once were rare, but have become more common in recent years. In such situations, it has become common for the majority leader to move to proceed to consider the measure, immediately submit a motion for cloture on his motion to proceed, and then immediately withdraw the motion to proceed. This proceeding permits the Senate to consider other business while the petition ripens, rather than having to extend debate on the motion to proceed. On the second following day, if the Senate defeats the motion for cloture, it continues with other business; if cloture is invoked, the action automatically brings back the motion to proceed as the pending business, but under the restrictions of cloture.

Sometimes an amendment provokes a filibuster even though the underlying bill does not. If cloture is invoked on the amendment, the operation of cloture is exhausted once the amendment is disposed of. Thereafter, debate on the bill continues, but under the general rules of the Senate. On occasion, cloture has been invoked, in this way, separately on several amendments to a bill in succession. Alternatively, cloture may be invoked on the bill itself, so that debate on the amendment continues under the restrictions of cloture on the overall measure. If the amendment is not germane to the bill, however, its supporters will oppose this approach, for (as discussed later) the cloture rule requires that amendments considered under cloture be germane. If cloture is invoked on a bill while a nongermane amendment is pending, the amendment becomes out of order and may not be further considered. In such a case it may be necessary instead to invoke cloture on the amendment, so as to secure a final vote on it, and then, after the amendment is disposed of, move for cloture on the bill as well.

After the Senate has passed a measure, additional action may be necessary in order that the Senate may go to conference with the House on the legislation. The motions necessary for this purpose are debatable, and as a result, supporters of the measure have occasionally found it necessary to move for cloture thereon. Conference reports themselves, unlike measures on initial consideration, are not subject to a double filibuster, because they are privileged matters, so that motions to proceed to their consideration are not debatable.[14] Inasmuch as conference reports themselves are debatable, however, it may be found necessary to move for cloture on a conference report.

Occasionally, cloture has also been sought on other debatable questions, such as:

- motions to waive the Budget Act,
- motions to recommit a measure with instructions that it be reported back forthwith with an amendment, or
- overriding a Presidential veto.

Timing of Cloture Motions

The relation of cloture motions to filibusters may depend on when the cloture motions are filed. Prior to the 1970s, consideration of a matter was usually allowed to proceed for some days or even weeks before cloture was sought, or cloture might not be sought at all. In more recent decades it has become common to seek cloture on a matter much earlier in the course of consideration, even immediately after consideration has begun. In some cases, a cloture motion has been filed, or has been deemed to have been filed, even before the matter in question has been called up. (Because the rules permit filing a motion for cloture only on a pending question, either of these actions, of course, requires unanimous consent.) When cloture is sought before any dilatory action actually occurs, the action may be an indication that the threat of a filibuster is present, or at least is thought to be present.

There often has been more than one cloture vote on the same question. If and when the Senate rejects a cloture motion, a Senator then can file a second motion to invoke cloture on that question. In some cases, Senators even have anticipated that a cloture motion may fail, so they have filed a second motion before the Senate has voted on the first one. For example, one cloture motion may be presented on Monday and another on Tuesday. If the Senate rejects the first motion when it matures on Wednesday, the second motion will ripen for a vote on Thursday. (If the Senate agrees to the first motion, there is no need, of course, for it to act on the second.) There have been instances in which there have been even more cloture votes on the same question. During the 100th Congress (1987-1988), for example, there were eight cloture votes, all unsuccessful, in connection with a campaign finance reform bill.

It also may be necessary for the Senate to attempt cloture on several different questions in order to complete consideration of a single measure. The possibility of having to obtain cloture first ona motion to proceed to consider a measure and subsequently also on the measure itself has already been discussed. Cloture on multiple questions may also be required when the Senate considers a bill with a pending amendment in the nature of a substitute. As already mentioned, once cloture has been invoked on a question, Rule XXII requires amendments to that question to be germane. As with other amendments, accordingly, if a pending amendment in the nature of a substitute contains provisions nongermane to the underlying bill, and the Senate proceeds to invoke cloture on the bill, further consideration of the substitute is rendered out of order. In such a case,bringing action to a conclusion may require obtaining cloture first on the substitute and then, once the substitute has been adopted, also on the underlying bill.

In current practice, it is not unusual for the majority leader to move for cloture on the underlying bill immediately after filing cloture on the amendment in the nature of a substitute. Under these circumstances, the two-day layover required for each cloture motion is being fulfilled simultaneously for both. The first cloture motion filed (on the amendment in the nature of a substitute) ripens first, at which point the Senate votes on that cloture motion. If cloture is invoked and after the Senate votes on adopting the substitute— after the possible 30 hours of post- cloture consideration—the second cloture motion (on the bill) is automatically pending, having already met the two-day layover.

EFFECTS OF INVOKING CLOTURE

Invoking cloture on a bill (or on any other question) does not produce an immediate vote on it. The effect of invoking cloture is only to guarantee that a vote will take place eventually.

Time for Consideration and Debate

Rule XXII imposes a cap of no more than 30 additional hours for the Senate to consider a question after invoking cloture on it. This 30-hour cap is a ceiling on the time available for post- cloture *consideration*, not just for *debate*. The time used in debate is counted against the 30 hours, but so too is the time consumed by quorum calls, roll call votes, parliamentary inquiries, and all other proceedings that occur while the matter under cloture is pending before the Senate. The 30- hour period can be increased if the Senate agrees to a non-debatable motion for that purpose. Adopting this motion also requires a three-fifths vote of the Senators duly chosen and sworn.

During the period for post-cloture consideration, each Senator is entitled to *speak* for a total of not more than one hour. Senators may yield part or all of their time to any of four others: the majority or minority leaders or the majority or minority floor managers. None of these Senators can accumulate more than two hours of additional time for debate; but, in turn, they can yield some or all of their time to others.[15]

There is insufficient time for all Senators to use their entire hour for debate within the 30-hour cap for post-cloture consideration. This disparity results from a 1985 amendment to the cloture rule. Before 1979, there was no cap at all on post-cloture consideration; the only restriction in Rule XXII was the limit of one hour per Senator for debate. The time consumed by reading amendments and conducting roll call votes and quorum calls was not deducted from anyone's hour. As a result, Senators could (and did) engage in what became known as post-cloture filibusters. By offering one amendment after another, for example, and demanding roll call votes to dispose of them, Senators could consume hours of the Senate's time while consuming little if any of their allotted hour for debate. In reaction, the Senate amended Rule XXII in 1979 to impose a 100-hour cap on post-cloture consideration. In theory, at least, this time period could accommodate the one hour of debate per Senator (but only if Senators used all of the 100 hours only for debate). Then, in 1985, the Senate agreed, without significant dissent, to reduce the 100 hours to 30 hours, while leaving unchanged the allocation of one hour for each Senator to debate.

The result is that there is not enough time available under cloture for each Senator to speak for an hour.[16] In principle, 30 Senators speaking for one hour each could consume all the time for post- cloture consideration. However, Rule XXII does provide a limited protection for all Senators by providing that, when the 30 hours expire, "any Senator who has not used or yielded at least ten minutes, is, if he seeks recognition, guaranteed up to ten minutes, inclusive, to speak only."[17]

Under these conditions, Senators may still be able to extend post-cloture consideration, but it typically would last little, if any, longer than the 30 hours available for consideration under cloture. Once cloture has imposed its definitive limit on further consideration, opponents sometimes see little benefit in the limited delay they might still obtain, and rather than insist on the use of the full 30 hours, they may instead permit a final vote well before the full time expires. In this case, the Senate may agree by unanimous consent that the 30 hours be considered to run continuously, even when the Senate is not actively considering the measure or even does not remain in session.

There is one other notable difference in the Senate's debate rules before and after cloture is invoked. As discussed above, Senate floor debate normally does not have to be germane, except when the Pastore rule applies. Under cloture, debate must be germane. This requirement derives from the language of Rule XXII that allows each Senator to speak for no more than one hour "on the measure, motion, or other matter pending before the Senate...." Senate precedents make clear that Senators should not expect the presiding officer to insist on germane debate at his or her initiative. Senators wishing to enforce the requirement that debate be germane can do so by making points of order from the floor.

Offering Amendments and Motions

There are several key restrictions governing the amendments that Senators can propose under cloture that do not apply to Senate floor amendments under most other circumstances. Some of these restrictions also apply to other motions Senators may offer, or actions they may take, under cloture.

Germane Amendments Only

Only germane amendments are eligible for floor consideration under cloture.[18] This germaneness requirement applies to the amendments that Senators offer after cloture is invoked, and the requirement applies as well to any amendments that were pending (that is, amendments that had been called up for consideration but were not yet disposed of) at the time that the Senate votes for cloture. Thus, immediately after a successful cloture vote, the majority leader or another Senator typically makes a point of order that one or more amendments that were pending when the vote began now must "fall" because they are not germane to the matter on which the Senate just invoked cloture.

This germaneness requirement helps explain why the Senate may have to invoke cloture on an amendment to a bill, and then invoke cloture again on the bill itself. It is quite common for a Senate committee to report a bill back to the Senate with an amendment in the nature of a substitute—a complete alternative for the text of the bill as introduced. The Senate almost always adopts this substitute immediately before voting to pass the bill as amended by the substitute. However, it also is not unusual for the committee substitute to be nongermane to the bill in some respect. Thus, if the Senate invokes cloture on the bill before it votes on the committee substitute, the substitute becomes out of order as nongermane, so that the Senate cannot agree to it. To protect the committee substitute (or any other nongermane amendment that the Senate is considering), the Senate can first invoke cloture on the amendment. Doing so limits further consideration of the amendment to no more than 30 more hours. If the Senate then adopts the amendment, cloture no longer is in effect, and Senators can filibuster the bill as amended. However, inasmuch as the previous nongermane amendment is now part of the text of the bill, it therefore cannot now be nongermane to the bill. At this point, therefore, the Senate may again vote to invoke cloture, this time on the bill as amended.

Any Senator can appeal the chair's ruling that a certain amendment is nongermane, allowing the Senate to overturn that ruling by simple majority vote. However, the Senate is unlikely to takethis action because doing so could fundamentally undermine the integrity and utility of the cloture procedure. In a sense, the decision to invoke cloture constitutes a kind of treaty by which Senators relinquish their right to filibuster in exchange for a guarantee that no nongermane amendments will be offered under cloture that some of those Senators would want to filibuster. Unless a Senator could be confident that, under cloture, his colleagues could not offer amendments on unrelated subjects that the Senator would insist on filibustering, that Senator would have serious qualms about ever voting for cloture. On some occasions when a Senator appealed a ruling of the chair under cloture that an amendment was not germane, Senators who may have supported the amendment on its merits nonetheless voted to sustain the ruling of the chair with the long-run viability of the cloture rule in mind.

Cloture is sometimes sought not for the purpose of overcoming a filibuster by debate, but primarily to trigger the requirement for germaneness of amendments. One way in which this situation can occur may arise when Senators wish to secure floor consideration for a bill that the majority party leadership is reluctant to schedule for floor consideration. Supporters of the billmay offer the text of that bill as a nongermane amendment to another bill that the majority party leadership is eager to pass. Opponents of the amendment may respond by moving for cloture on the bill, then prolonging the debate so as to prevent a vote on the amendment until the time comes for voting on the cloture motion. If the Senate votes to invoke cloture, the nongermane amendment is subject to a point of order. In this way, its opponents can dispose of the amendment adversely without ever having to vote on it, or even on a motion to table it — but only, of course, if they can mobilize three-fifths of the Senate to vote for cloture. This possibility, which is more than hypothetical, illustrates that not every cloture vote takes place to overcome a filibuster that is already in progress.

Amendments Submitted in Writing

To be in order under cloture, amendments must be submitted at the desk in writing (and for printing in the *Congressional Record*) before the cloture vote takes place.[19] There are different requirements for first-degree amendments (amendments to change the text of a bill or resolution) and second-degree amendments (amendments to change the text of a pending first-degree amendment). Under Rule XXII,

> Except by unanimous consent, no amendment shall be proposed after the vote to bring the debate to a close, unless it had been submitted in writing to the Journal Clerk by 1 o'clock p.m. on the day following the filing of the cloture motion if an amendment in the first degree, and unless it had been so submitted at least one hour prior to the beginning of the cloture vote if an amendment in the second degree.

Senators sometimes submit a large number of amendments to a bill for printing in the *Congressional Record* even before a cloture motion is presented. In some cases, this may be understood or intended as a signal that the Senators who submitted the amendments for printing are contemplating a filibuster.

In practice, the deadline in Rule XXII usually gives Senators most or all of a day after cloture is proposed to draft germane amendments to the bill. Senators then usually have most or all of the next day to review those first-degree amendments and to decide what second-degree amendments, if any, they might offer to them. In this way, Senators can be fully aware of all the amendments they may encounter under cloture before they vote on whether or not to invoke cloture. (Submitting an amendment in writing does not exempt that amendment from the restriction that only germane amendments are in order under cloture.)

Rule XXII establishes no separate deadline for submitting amendments in the nature of a substitute (i.e., substitutes for the full text of a measure), which are amendable in two degrees— that is, an amendment to an amendment in the nature of a substitute is a first-degree amendment.[20] An amendment in the nature of a substitute might be submitted at any time up to the deadline for first-degree amendments. If it were submitted just before that deadline, Senators might have essentially no time to prepare amendments to it, because they, as first-degree amendments, would be subject to the same deadline as the substiturte.

One result of these requirements is that, whenever cloture is proposed, Senators and their staffs must decide whether they need to prepare and submit amendments to the measure. When the Senate has voted to invoke cloture on a bill, it is too late for a Senator then to think about what amendments to the bill he or she might want to propose. When a cloture motion is filed, Senators often conclude that they need to proceed with drafting whatever amendments they might want to offer, on the assumption that the Senate will approve the motion two days later. One result is that there often are significantly more amendments submitted for printing in the *Record* than Senators actually offer after cloture is invoked.

Under cloture, a Senator may not modify an amendment that he or she has offered. Permitting modifications would be inconsistent with the principle implicit in the cloture rule that Senators should be able to know what amendments may be offered under cloture before the Senate decides if it will invoke cloture. In addition, if an amendment is submitted and called up after a cloture motion is filed, and is then modified while the cloture motion is pending, the amendment becomes out of order, and falls, because the amendment, in its modified form, did not meet the filing deadline for an amendment to be considered under cloture.

Rule XXII permits only one limited circumstance in which Senators are allowed to change the amendments they offer under cloture. If a measure or other matter is reprinted for some reason after the Senate has invoked cloture on it and if the reprinting changes page and line numbers, amendments that otherwise are in order will remain in order and can be reprinted to makeconforming changes in page and line numbering.

Multiple Amendments

Rule XXII states that "[n]o Senator shall call up more than two amendments until every other Senator shall have had the opportunity to do likewise." The evident purpose of this provision is to prevent some Senators from dominating the Senate's proceedings under cloture. This restriction, which Senators have rarely if ever chosen to enforce, does not create a significant problem for those wishing to consume the time available for post-cloture consideration. From their perspective, what is most important is that amendments be offered, not who offers them.

Dilatory Amendments and Motions

Rule XXII provides that no dilatory motion or amendment is in order under cloture. Furthermore, the Senate has established precedents that empower the presiding officer to rule motions and amendments out of order as dilatory without Senators first making points of order to that effect from the floor. Presiding officers rarely have exercised this authority. On occasion, however, and whether at their own initiative or in response to points of order, presiding officers have ruled amendments and various kinds of motions to be dilatory and, therefore, not in order.[21] For example, motions to adjourn, postpone, recess, and reconsider have been held to be dilatory. There also is precedent supporting the authority of the presiding officer to rule that a quorum call is dilatory.

Under normal Senate procedures, appeals from rulings of the chair usually are debatable (though they also are subject to tabling motions). Under cloture, however, appeals are not debatable. In extraordinary circumstances, appeals from rulings of the chair have even been ruled out of order as dilatory.[22]

Reading and Division of Amendments

Under normal Senate procedure, each amendment that is offered must be read before debate on it may begin, unless the reading is waived by unanimous consent, as it usually is. Under Rule XXII, however, the reading of any amendment automatically is waived if it "has been available in printed form at the desk of the Members for not less than twenty-four hours." This requirement usually is satisfied because amendments considered under cloture must have been submitted for printing before the cloture vote.

Also, under normal Senate procedure any Senator can demand that an amendment be divided into two or more component parts if each part could stand as an independent proposition (but amendments in the form of motions to strike out and insert are not divisible). Under cloture, however, a Senator cannot demand as a matter of right that an amendment be divided.[23]

The Authority of the Presiding Officer

When the Senate is operating under cloture, the Senate's presiding officer has powers that he or she does not have under the Senate's regular procedures. Under normal Senate procedure, in particular, the chair is not empowered to count whether a quorum is present on the floor. When a Senator suggests the absence of a quorum, the chair's only response is to direct the clerk to call the roll. Under cloture, however, the presiding officer can count to ascertain the presence of a quorum.

Under cloture, as well, the presiding officer may rule amendments and motions out of order at his or her own initiative, without waiting for Senators to make a point of order from the floor.[24] In current practice, however, as noted earlier, nongermane and dilatory amendments typically fall on a point of order made by the majority leader immediately after cloture has been invoked.

Business on the Senate Floor

Cloture also affects the consequences of a filibuster for other legislative and executive business that the Senate could conduct. Rule XXII provides that once the Senate invokes cloture, "then said measure, motion or other matter pending before the Senate, or the unfinished business, shall be the unfinished business to the exclusion of all other business until disposed of." If the Senate invokes cloture on a bill, in other words, the rule requires the body to continue to consider that bill until it completes action on it.

The Rule provides no mechanism for the Senate to set aside the matter being considered under cloture, even temporarily, in order to consider other matters, even those that are of an emergency nature or far less contentious. As a result, a filibuster can affect the fate not only of the matter that provokes it, but also other matters that the Senate may not be able to consider (or at least not as soon as it would like) because of the filibuster. In practice, however, the Senate often provides by unanimous consent for the consideration of other matters. Arrangements of this kind permit the Senate to accomplish necessary routine business, or make progress on other matters, at the same time as it continues to move toward a final resolution of the matter on which it has invoked cloture.

THE IMPACT OF FILIBUSTERS

Obviously, a filibuster has the greatest impact on the Senate when a 60-vote majority cannot be assembled to invoke cloture. In that case, the measure or other matter that is being filibustered is doomed unless its opponents relent and allow the Senate to vote on it. Even if cloture is invoked, however, a filibuster can significantly affect how, when, and even whether the Senate conducts its legislative and executive business. In fact, it is not an exaggeration to say that filibusters and the prospect of filibusters shape much of the way in which the Senate does its work on the floor.

Impact on the Time for Consideration

In principle, a truly determined minority of Senators, even one too small to prevent cloture, usually can delay for as much as two weeks the time at which the Senate finally votes to pass a bill that most Senators support. **Table 1** summarizes a hypothetical example. In this example, a motion to proceed to the bill's consideration is made on a Monday (Day 1). If a filibuster on that motion is begun or is anticipated, proponents of the motion and the bill can present a cloture motion on the same day. However, under Rule XXII, the cloture vote on the motion to proceed does not take place until Wednesday (Day 3). Assuming the Senate invokes cloture on Wednesday, there then begins the 30-hour period for post-cloture consideration of the motion. If the Senate is in session for eight hours per day, Monday through Friday, the 30-hour period, if fully consumed, will extend over almost four full days of session, or at least until the end of the Senate's session on the following Monday (Day 6). If, at that time, the Senate votes for the motion to proceed, the bill's opponents then may begin to filibuster the bill itself, requiring another cloture motion, another successful cloture vote (on Day 8), and the expiration of another 30-hour period for post-cloture consideration. Under these conditions, Rule XXII would require that the vote on final passage occur on the 11th day of consideration, or the 15th calendar day after the motion to proceed was made.

Table 1. Time That May Be Required for Senate Action in a Typical Cloture Situation

Senate action	Cumulative days consumed	
	Days of session	Calendar days
Motion to proceed made	1	1
Cloture motion filed on motion to proceed	1	1
Vote on invoking cloture on motion to proceed	3	3
Vote on motion to proceed	6	8
Cloture motion filed on measure	6	8
Vote on invoking cloture on measure	8	10
Vote on final passage of measure	11	15

How long an actual filibuster can delay final Senate action may be affected by the answers that can be given, in the individual case, to many questions. These include:

- Is cloture proposed as soon as the motion to proceed is made, and then again as soon as possible after the Senate takes up the bill (after having agreed to the motion to proceed)?
- Can the bill's supporters secure the 60 votes needed to agree to the first cloture motion on the motion to proceed, or is more than one attempt necessary before the Senate votes for cloture on the motion?
- Similarly, does the Senate adopt the first cloture motion on the bill itself, or is cloture invoked on the bill only on a second or subsequent attempt?

- Can the Senate agree by unanimous consent to expedite the process by providing for votes on cloture before the time specified in Rule XXII?
- Are the bill's opponents willing and able to consume the entire 30-hour period for post-cloture consideration of the motion to proceed, and also the same amount of time for post-cloture consideration of the bill?
- After the Senate invokes cloture, for how many days, and for how many hours per day, is the Senate in session to consider the bill?
- Does the Senate meet late into the evening, or all night, or on the weekend, in order to consume both 30-hour periods more quickly than it otherwise would? Or can unanimous consent be obtained that the 30-hour periods run continuously?

Although the actual time consumed varies from case to case, clearly filibusters can create significant delays, even when there are 60-vote majorities to invoke cloture. How much delay the Senate experiences depends in part on how much time the Senate, and especially its majority party leadership, is prepared to devote to the bill in question. If the bill is particularly important to the nation and to the majority party's legislative agenda, for example, the majority leader may be willing to invest the days or even weeks that can be necessary to withstand and ultimately end a filibuster.

Another consideration is the point in the annual session and in the biennial life of a Congress at which a filibuster takes place. In the first months of the first session, for example, there may be relatively little business that is ready for Senate floor consideration. In that case, the Senate may be able to endure an extended filibuster without sacrificing its ability to act in a timely way on other legislation. Toward the end of each session, however, and especially as the Senate approaches *sine die* adjournment at the end of the second session, time becomes increasingly scarce and precious. Every hour and every day of floor time that one bill consumes is time that is not available for the Senate to act on other measures that will die if not enacted into law beforethe end of the Congress. Therefore, the costs of filibusters increase because their effects on the legislative prospects of other bills become greater and greater.

The Prospect of a Filibuster

However much effect filibusters have on the operations of the Senate, perhaps a more pervasive effect is attributable to filibusters that have not taken place—at least not yet. In many instances, cloture motions may be filed not to overcome filibusters in progress, but to preempt ones that are only anticipated. Also, the prospect of a filibuster often affects when or whether the Senate will consider a measure on the floor, and how the Senate will consider it.

Holds

A Senator who does not want the Senate to consider a certain measure or matter, whether temporarily or permanently, could monitor the Senate floor and then object if and when the majority leader proposes to call up the question for consideration. The practice of placing holds on measures or matters, however, has developed informally as a way for Senators to interpose such an objection in advance and without having to do so in person on the floor. For a Senator to place a hold is for the Senator to request that the majority leader not even try to call up the measure for consideration, at least not without giving advance notice to the Senator who has placed the hold.

This request has no formal standing in Senate rules, and is not binding on the leader. Fundamentally, however, when a Senator places the hold, he or she is implicitly registering his or her intention to object to any unanimous consent request for consideration of the measure or matter. In turn, the majority leader and the measure's prospective floor manager understand that a Senator who objects to allowing a bill or resolution to be called up by unanimous consent may back up his or her objection by filibustering a motion to proceed to its consideration.[25] Recent majority leaders have accordingly tended to honor holds, both as a courtesy to their colleagues, and in recognition that if they choose not to do so, they may well confront filibusters that they prefer to avoid.

In this way, the threat of a filibuster often is sufficient to prevent a measure or matter from coming to the Senate floor. At a minimum, a bill's supporters may discuss with the Senators making the threat whether the bill can be amended in a way that satisfies their concerns and removes any danger of a filibuster. Even if the bill's proponents are satisfied that they could invoke cloture on the bill, they still may be willing to accept unwelcome amendments to the bill in order to avoid a protracted process of floor consideration. In fact, depending on the importance of the bill and the other measures that await floor action, the majority leader may be reluctant toschedule the bill (or other matter) unless he is assured that the Senate can complete action on it without undue delay.

Linkage and Leverage

As noted above, sometimes a filibuster or the threat of a filibuster can affect the prospects of other measures or matters simply by compelling the Senate to devote so much time to the filibustered matter that there is insufficient time available to take up all the other measures that it otherwise would consider and pass. Senators also have been known to use their rights under Rule XXII to delay action on a bill or item of executive business as leverage to secure the action (or inaction) they want on another, unrelated question.

Suppose, for example, that a Senator opposes S. 1, but knows that he or she lacks the support to filibuster against it effectively. A Senator in this situation may not have enough leverage to prevent Senate floor consideration of S. 1 or to secure satisfactory changes in the bill. So the Senator may seek to increase his or her leverage by delaying, or threatening to delay, the Senate's consideration of other bills that are scheduled for floor action before S. 1. By threatening to filibuster S. 2, S. 3, and S. 4, for example, or by actually delaying their consideration, the Senator may strengthen his or her bargaining position by making it clear that more is at stake than the prospects and provisions of S. 1. In this way, Senators' opposition to one bill can affect the Senate's floor agenda in unexpected and unpredictable ways.

Consensus

More generally, the possibility of filibusters creates a powerful incentive for Senators to strive for legislative consensus. The votes of only a majority of Senators present and voting are needed to pass a bill on the floor. It can, however, require the votes of 60 Senators to invoke cloture on the bill in order to overcome a filibuster and enable the Senate to reach that vote on final passage. Knowing this, a bill's supporters have good reason to write it in a way that will attract the support of at least three-fifths of all Senators.

What is more, there often are more bills that are ready to be considered on the Senate floor than there is time available for acting on them. Under these circumstances, the majority leader may be reluctant, especially toward the end of a Congress, even to call up a bill unless he can be assured that it will not be filibustered. The threat of a filibuster may be enough to convince the majority leader to devote the Senate's time to other matters instead, even if all concerned agree that the filibuster ultimately would not succeed in preventing the Senate from passing the bill.

In such a case, a bill's supporters may not be content with securing the support of even 60 Senators. In the hope of eliminating the threat of a filibuster, the proponents may try to accommodate the interests of all Senators, or at least to convince them that a good faith effort has been made to assuage their concerns. At best, opponents can become supporters. At worst, opponents may remain opposed, but may decide against expressing their opposition through a filibuster. While true consensus on major legislative issues may be impossible, the dynamics of the Senate's legislative process do promote efforts to come as close to consensus as the strongly held beliefs of Senators permit.

KEY POLICY STAFF

Area of Expertise	Name	Phone	E-mail
Senate floor procedure	Richard S. Beth	7-8667	rbeth@crs.loc.gov
Senate floor procedure	Christopher M. Davis	7-0656	cmdavis@crs.loc.gov
Senate floor procedure	Valerie Heitshusen	7-8635	vheitshusen@crs.loc.gov
Senate floor procedure	Walter Oleszek	7-7854	woleszek@crs.loc.gov
Senate floor procedure	Betsy Palmer	7-0381	bpalmer@crs.loc.gov

End Notes

[1] U.S. Congress, Senate, *Riddick's Senate Procedure: Precedents and Practices*, S.Doc. 101-28, 101st Cong., 2nd sess., by Floyd M. Riddick, Parliamentarian Emeritus, and Alan S. Frumin, Parliamentarian, rev. and ed. by Alan S. Frumin (Washington: GPO, 1992), pp. 282-334.

[2] The record for the longest single speech remains that made by Sen. Strom Thurmond of South Carolina on Aug. 28-29, 1957, which consumed 24 hours and 18 minutes. U.S. Senate, Committee on Rules and Administration, *Senate Cloture Rule*, committee print, 99th Cong., 1st sess., S.Prt. 99-95 (Washington: GPO, 1985), p. 40.

[3] "Therefore, the two speech rule requires not a mechanical test, but the application of the rule of reason." *Riddick's Senate Procedure*, pp. 782-783.

[4] Franklin Burdette, *Filibustering in the Senate* (New York: Russell & Russell, 1965; reprint of 1940 Princeton University Press edition), p. 4.

[5] *Riddick's Senate Procedure*, p. 755.

[6] Senators sometimes ask unanimous consent to yield to a colleague for something other than a question without losing their right to the floor. Any Senator can object to this request.

[7] *Riddick's Senate Procedure*, p. 1053. On what constitutes intervening business, see pp. 1042-1046.

[8] The Senate, unlike the House, does not use an electronic voting system.

[9] "[T]he sufficiency of the number of Senators demanding a roll call is based on the last preceding roll call. The Chair, noting that 81 Senators had just voted, denied the yeas and nays when only 16 Senators responded to a request for a sufficient second. A demand for the yeas and nays immediately following a call of the Senate is seconded by one-fifth of those answering such call, or immediately following a yea and nay vote, seconded by one-fifth of those voting." *Riddick's Senate Procedure*, p. 1417.

[10] If the Senate stays in session beyond midnight on the day after the cloture motion is filed, the cloture vote does not occur one hour into the second calendar day of session. For detail, see *Riddick's Senate Procedure*, p. 330.

[11] Rule XXII, paragraph 2.

[12] Committee on Rules and Administration, *Senate Cloture Rule*, pp. 119-121.

[13] Senate Rule VII, paragraph 2, and Senate Rule VIII, paragraph 2. Although Senate Rules do not restrict who may offer a motion to proceed, the Senate normally accords the majority leader the prerogative of doing so, in pursuance of his functions of arranging the floor agenda. *Riddick's Senate Procedure*, p. 655. Even in the equally divided Senate of the 107th Cong., the "power-sharing agreement" (S.Res. 8, adopted Jan. 5, 2001) affirmed this practice.

[14] Similarly, no debate is allowed on a motion that the Senate go into executive session to consider a particular nomination or treaty.

[15] Hypothetically, therefore, one Senator could control a maximum of 13 hours for debate. This would require eight Senators to yield all of their time to the four designated party leaders and floor managers (two Senators yielding their time to one of the four), giving each party leader and floor manager control of three hours apiece. If the four designated Senators then yielded all of their combined 12 hours to a fifth Senator, who controls one hour in his or her own right, that Senator would control 13 hours.

[16] When one Senator yields to another for a question, the time required to ask the question comes out of the hour controlled by the Senator who yielded.

[17] When a Senator has consumed all of his or her hour for debate, that Senator may continue to offer amendments, but has no time to explain them. At the end of the 30 hours for post-cloture consideration, no further amendments may be offered.

[18] On what constitutes a germane amendment, see *Riddick's Senate Procedure*, pp. 291-294.

[19] A Senator can call up an amendment that another Senator had submitted in writing, though Senators rarely do so. Also, a Senator may recall amendments that he or she submitted in writing before a cloture vote. By recalling an amendment, the Senator removes it from potential consideration under cloture.

[20] *Riddick's Senate Procedure*, p. 88.

[21] Amendments that only express the sense of the Senate or the sense of Congress (and, therefore, would not have the force of law if enacted) have been considered dilatory *per se* under cloture. No other type of amendment has been held to be dilatory *per se* under cloture.

[22] In 1982, the presiding officer stated that "the right to appeal is a basic right of each Senator and would be held dilatory only in the most extraordinary circumstances." *Riddick's Senate Procedure*, p. 312.

[23] An amendment that was offered and divided before the cloture vote continues to be considered as divided after cloture is invoked.

[24] *Riddick's Senate Procedure*, p. 287.

[25] As implied by references to both measures and matters, a hold may be placed on a piece of legislation (bill or resolution) or on another matter (an item of executive business – i.e., a nomination or treaty). However, a motion to proceed to consideration of an item of executive business that is on the Calendar is not subject to debate. (Executive business items are typically taken up by unanimous consent, but could, alternatively, be brought up via a nondebatable motion to proceed to such an item.) Thus, holds on legislation are typically understood as an objection to proceeding to a bill or resolution; a hold on an item of executive business is understood to embody a threat of extended debate on the item itself. Even in the latter situation, a hold on a nomination itself, for example, could have the same effect on the nomination as a hold on a bill; that is, the majority leader may decide not to try to proceed to it, based on the hold.

In: Filibusters, Cloture and Holds in the Senate   ISBN: 978-1-61728-925-5
Editors: David J. Gilgram   © 2010 Nova Science Publishers, Inc.

Chapter 2

CLOTURE ATTEMPTS ON NOMINATIONS[*]

Richard S. Beth and Betsy Palmer

SUMMARY

Cloture is the only means by which the Senate can vote to limit debate on a matter, and thereby overcome a possible filibuster. It would be erroneous, however, to assume that cases in which cloture is sought are the same as those in which a filibuster occurs. Cloture may be sought when no filibuster is taking place, and filibusters may occur without cloture being sought.

Until 1949, cloture could not be invoked on nominations, and before 1980 this action was attempted only twice. From the 96th Congress (1979-1980) through the 102nd (199 1-1992), cloture was never sought on more than three nominations in a single Congress, but since then this level has been exceeded four times.

From 1949 through 2008, cloture was sought on 68 nominations, and invoked on 31. The Senate voted to reject cloture on 20 of the remaining 37 nominations, and on the final 17 nominations no cloture motion received a vote. Seventeen of the 68 nominees failed of confirmation, and 11 of these 17 were considered during the 108th Congress (2003-2004). In the 103rd Congress (1993- 1994) and the 109th Congress (2005-2006) most of the cloture attempts

---

[*] This is an edited, reformatted and augmented version of a CRS Report for Congress publication dated March 2009.

were to executive branch nominations, but in all other Congresses nominations to the federal bench predominated.

Cloture has been sought on four nominations to the Supreme Court. In 1968, a cloture vote on the motion to proceed to consider the nomination of Abe Fortas to be Chief Justice failed. In 1971, when he was first appointed to the court, and again in 1986 when he was nominated to be Chief Justice, opponents of William H. Rehnquist mounted a filibuster. Though the cloture vote in 1971 was unsuccessful, Rehnquist was confirmed to the court; in 1986, the cloture vote was successful. In 2006, the Senate successfully invoked cloture on the nomination of Samuel A. Alito, Jr., to be an associate justice on the Supreme Court.

CLOTURE, FILIBUSTERS, AND HOW THEY DIFFER

Senate Rules place no general limits on how long consideration of a nomination (or most other matters) may last. Owing to this lack of general time limits, opponents of a nomination may be able to use extended debate or other delaying actions to prevent a final vote from occurring. Although a voting majority of Senators may be prepared to vote for a nominee, the nomination cannot be confirmed as long as other Senators, presumably a voting minority, are able to prevent the vote from occurring. The use of debate and procedural actions for the purpose of preventing or delaying a vote is a filibuster.

The motion for cloture is the only procedure by which the Senate can vote to place time limits on its consideration of a matter. It is, therefore, the Senate's most usual means of attempting to overcome a filibuster. When the Senate adopts a cloture motion on a matter, known as "invoking cloture," further consideration of the matter is limited to 30 hours.[1] By invoking cloture, the Senate may be able to ensure that a question will ultimately come to a vote, and can be decided by a voting majority.

The cloture rule permits Senators to move for cloture repeatedly, if necessary. The Senate, however, can impose the constraints of cloture only by a super-majority vote. For most matters, including nominations, three-fifths of the full Senate, or 60 votes, is required to invoke cloture. As a result, even if a majority of Senators support a nomination, opponents may still be able to prevent a vote on it by defeating any attempt to invoke cloture. Although the nomination itself can always be approved by a simple majority of Senators present and voting, the support of a super-majority may be required to limit consideration and enable the Senate to reach a vote.

While cloture affords the Senate a means of overcoming a filibuster, it is erroneous to assume that cases in which cloture is sought are always the same as those in which a filibuster occurs. Cloture may be sought when no filibuster is taking place, and filibusters may occur without cloture being sought. The reason is that cloture is sought by supporters of a matter, while filibusters are conducted by its opponents. Leaders of the majority party, or other supporters, may move for cloture even when opponents do not assert that they are attempting a filibuster, or when no extended debate or delaying actions have actually occurred. They may do so in response to a threat or perceived threat of a filibuster, or simply in an effort to speed action.

It is also possible for opponents of a matter to engage in a filibuster without supporters deciding to move for cloture. Supporters may refrain either because they think they lack the votes to obtain cloture, because they believe they can overcome any delaying actions and reach a vote without cloture, or because they hope to resolve the matter in dispute by some negotiated accommodation. This situation may be less common today, but does seem to have occurred in relation to nominations in earlier times.

If cloture is not an automatic indicator of a filibuster, neither is any other specific procedural action. A filibuster is a matter of intent; any course of action by opponents of a matter may be a filibuster if it is undertaken with the purpose of blocking or delaying a vote. Yet any of the procedural actions that might be used to delay or block a vote might also be used for other purposes. As a result, filibusters cannot simply be identified by explicit or uniform criteria, and there is no commonly accepted set of criteria for doing so. Instead, determining whether a filibuster is occurring in any specific case typically requires a degree of subjective judgment.

For these reasons, it would be a misuse of the following data, identifying nominations on which cloture was sought, to treat them as identifying nominations subjected to filibuster. It would equally be a misinterpretation to assume that all nominations on which cloture was not sought were not filibustered (especially for periods before 1949, when it was first made possible to move cloture on nominations, as described in the next section). This chapter provides data only on nominations on which cloture motions were offered. It is not to be taken as providing systematic data on nominations that were or were not filibustered. It would not be feasible to develop a list of measures filibustered unless a commonly accepted single standard for identifying what constitutes filibustering could first be established.[2] At most, the data presented here may be regarded as identifying some potentially likely cases in which a filibuster (by some appropriate definition) may have occurred.

FREQUENCY OF CLOTURE ATTEMPTS ON NOMINATIONS

The Senate first adopted a cloture rule in 1917. Until 1949, cloture could be moved only on legislative measures, and nominations could not be subjected to cloture attempts.[3] From 1949 through 2008 (81st-110th Congresses), cloture was sought on 68 nominations.[4] Table 4, following the text of this chapter, identifies the 68 nominations, the number of separate cloture motions filed on each, the ultimate outcome of the cloture attempt in each case, and the disposition of each nomination. As shown by the summary in Table 1, the Senate invoked cloture on 31 of these 68 nominations. On another 17 nominations, cloture motions were offered, but never came to a vote, because the motions fell, were withdrawn or vitiated. On the remaining 20 nominations, the Senate voted against imposing cloture.[5]

Of the 68 nominations on which cloture was sought, 51 ultimately won confirmation. The 51 nominations confirmed include all 31 on which the Senate invoked cloture and 16 of those on which the Senate did not vote on the cloture motions, as well as four on which the Senate rejected cloture. The remaining 17 nominations were not confirmed, either because the Senate voted to reject cloture or because they did not receive a final vote. On 16 of these nominations, 11 of which occurred in the 108th Congress (2003-2004), the Senate rejected cloture. In the final case in the 109th Congress (2006-2007), the cloture motion was withdrawn and the nomination was not confirmed. Before the 108th Congress, only three of the 35 nominations on which cloture was sought were ultimately rejected. These were

Table 1. Cloture Attempts and Action on Nominations

Cloture Action	Action on Nomination		Total
	Confirmed	Not confirmed	
Invoked	31	0	31
Rejected	4	16	20
Withdrawn/Vitiated/Fell[a]	16	1	17
Total	51	17	68

- Justice Abe Fortas to be Chief Justice of the United States in 1968;
- Sam Brown to be Ambassador during his tenure as Head of Delegation to the Conference on Security and Cooperation in Europe (CSCE) in 1994; and
- Dr. Henry Foster to be Surgeon General of the United States in 1995.

HISTORICAL DEVELOPMENT OF CLOTURE ATTEMPTS ON NOMINATIONS

Even after Senate rules began to permit cloture on nominations in 1949, cloture was sought on none until 1968, when a motion to proceed to consider the nomination of Supreme Court Associate Justice Abe Fortas to be Chief Justice was debated at length. After the Senate rejected cloture on the motion to proceed, 45-43, President Lyndon B. Johnson withdrew the nomination at Fortas' request. In 1969 and 1970, the nominations of Clement F. Haynsworth and G. Harrold Carswell to the Supreme Court were defeated after lengthy debate, but no cloture motion was filed on either. When the Senate considered the nomination to the Supreme Court of William H. Rehnquist late in the 1971 session, however, cloture was quickly sought. Though the Senate did not invoke cloture (52-42), the nomination was subsequently confirmed.

Table 2. Frequency and Success of Cloture Attempts on Nominations, by Time Period, 1949-2008

Congresses and (years)	Nominations on which cloture was:			
	Moved		Invoked	
	Number	Average per Congress	Number	Percent of moved
81st-89th (1949-1966)	0	0	0	—
90th-102nd (1967-1992)	12	0.9	9	75%
103rd-110th (1993-2008)	56	7.0	22	39%

In 1975, the majority required for invoking cloture on most matters, including nominations, was changed from two-thirds of Senators present and voting to three-fifths of the full membership of the Senate (normally 60).[6] This change in the rules generally meant that the threshold for invoking cloture was lowered; if all 100 Senators participated in the vote, the previous rule required the votes of 67 to invoke cloture, the new rule required 60 votes, regardless of how many Senators participated.

Cloture was sought on no other nomination until 1980. That occurrence was the first in which cloture was sought on a nomination to an executive branch position, that of William G. Lubbers to be General Counsel of the National Labor Relations Board. Cloture was invoked, and the nomination was confirmed.

As Table 2 illustrates, the frequency with which cloture has been sought on nominations has increased in recent years (a development that reflects the trend in the overall frequency of cloture motions). Before the 103rd Congress, cloture was sought on as many as three nominations only in the 96th Congress (1979-1980) and the 99th Congress (1985-1986). Since then, however, this level has been exceeded four times. Cloture was sought on 12 nominations in the 103rd Congress (1993-1994), five in the 107th (2001-2002), 14 in the 108th (2003-2004) and 18 in the 109th Congress (2005-2006). These four Congresses were also the only ones since 1981 in which the presidency, Senate, and House were all controlled by the same political party.[7] In addition, the 103rd and 107th Congresses were each the first of a new presidency, so that the number of nominations to be considered was presumably especially large.

Table 2 also indicates that, as the frequency of cloture attempts on nominations has increased, the frequency of their success has tended to decrease. This relationship appears to suggest that cloture is now being sought more often in cases when it is unlikely to be invoked. This shift was evident especially in the 103rd Congress, when cloture was successfully invoked on only four of the 12 nominations where attempted, and in the 108th Congress, when it was invoked on none of the 14 nominations on which it was attempted. In other Congresses, the proportion of cloture attempts that succeeded has generally been much higher.

In the 108th Congress (2003-2004), the pattern of Senate action on nominations on which cloture was sought displayed several distinctive features. First, the maximum number of cloture motions offered on any nomination was higher than in any other Congress.

Table 3. Cloture Action on Judicial and Executive Nominations, by Time Period, 1967-2008

Congresses and (years)	Judicial			Executive		
	Cloture Invoked	Cloture Rejected	Cloture Fell, Vitiated or Withdrawn[a]	Cloture Invoked	Cloture Rejected	Cloture Fell, Vitiated or Withdrawn[a]
90th-102nd (1967-1992)	5	2	1	4	0	0
103rd (1993-1994)	1	0	1	3	3	4
104th-107th (1995-2002)	5	1	1	3	1	0
108th (2003-2004)	0	10	2	0	1	1
109th (2005-2006)	6	0	0	3	2	7
110th (2007-2008)	1	0	0	0	0	0
Total	18	13	5	13	7	12

Source: Table 4.

Notes: All nominations on which cloture was invoked were confirmed. Four of the nominations for which cloture was rejected were confirmed. All but one of the nominations on which the cloture motion fell, was vitiated or withdrawn were ultimately confirmed. See Table 1.

a. This category only includes situations in which there was no vote on any cloture motion.

In other Congresses, as many as three cloture motions had been offered on a single nomination only on three occasions (two in 1980 and one in 1994). In the 108th Congress, by contrast, one nomination was subjected to seven cloture motions and another to four. Second, when the Senate sought cloture on a nomination but was unable to confirm it, the Senate in the 108th Congress retained the nomination on its calendar until final adjournment. In earlier Congresses, nominations that were not confirmed after cloture attempts were typically either withdrawn or returned to the President. Both these shifts may represent indications of an increased intensity with which supporters of these nominations were attempting to secure Senate votes on them.

Table 4. Nominations Subjected to Cloture Attempts, 1968-2008

Congress and Year	Nominee	Position	Number of Cloture Attempts[a]	Final Outcome of Cloture Attempt	Disposition of Nomination
90th, 1968	*Abe Fortas*	*Chief Justice*	*1*	**rejected**	**withdrawn**
92nd, 1971	*William H. Rehnquist*	*Associate Justice*	*2*	**rejected**	**confirmed**
96th, 1980	William A. Lubbers	General Counsel, National Labor Relations Board	3	invoked	confirmed
96th, 1980	Don Zimmerman	Member, National Labor Relations Board	3	invoked	confirmed
96th, 1980	*Stephen G. Breyer*	*Circuit Judge*	*2*	*invoked*	*confirmed*
98th, 1984	*J. Harvie Wilkinson*	*Circuit Judge*	*2*	*invoked*	confirmed
99th, 1986	*Sidney A. Fitzwater*	*District Judge*	*1*	*invoked*	confirmed
99th, 1986	*Daniel A. Manion*	*Circuit Judge*	*1*	*withdrawn*	confirmed
99th, 1986	*William H. Rehnquist*	*Chief Justice*	*1*	*invoked*	confirmed
100th, 1987	Melissa Wells	Ambassador	1	invoked	confirmed
100th, 1987	C. William Verity	Secretary of Commerce	1	invoked	confirmed
102nd, 1992	*Edward Earl Carnes, Jr.*	*Circuit Judge*	*1*	*invoked*	*confirmed*
103rd, 1993	*Walter Dellinger*	Assistant Attorney General	2	**rejected**	confirmed
103rd, 1993	*five nominations*[b]	State Department	2	**rejected**	confirmed
103rd, 1993	Janet Napolitano	U.S. Attorney	1	invoked	confirmed
103rd, 1994	M. Larry Lawrence	Ambassador	1	fell[b]	confirmed
103rd, 1994	*Rosemary Barkett*	*Circuit Judge*	*1*	*withdrawn*	*confirmed*

Table 4. (Continued)

Congress and Year	Nominee	Position	Number of Cloture Attempts[a]	Final Outcome of Cloture Attempt	Disposition of Nomination
103rd, 1994	Sam Brown	Ambassador	3	**rejected**	**returned to president**
103rd, 1994	Derek Shearer	Ambassador	2	invoked	confirmed
103rd, 1994	Ricki Tigert	Board Member and Chair, Federal Deposit Insurance Corporation c	2	invoked	confirmed
103rd, 1994	*H. Lee Sarokin*	*Circuit Judge*	*1*	*invoked*	*confirmed*
103rd, 1994	Buster Glosson	Air Force Lieutenant	1	withdrawn	confirmed
103rd, 1994	Claude Bolton, Jr.	General (retired) Air Force Brigadier General	1	vitiated[d]	confirmed
103rd, 1994	Edward P. Barry, Jr.	Air Force Lieuten-ant General (retired)	1	vitiated[d]	confirmed
104th, 1995	Henry Foster	Surgeon General	2	rejected	**no final vote**
105th, 1997	Joel I. Klein	Assistant Attorney General	1	invoked	confirmed
105th, 1998	David Satcher	Surgeon General	1	invoked	confirmed
106th, 1999	*Brian Thea-dore Stewart*	*District Judge*	*1*	***rejected***	*confirmed*
106th, 2000	*Marsha L. Berzon*	*Circuit Judge*	*1*	*invoked*	*confirmed*
106th, 2000	*Richard A. Paez*	*Circuit Judge*	*1*	*invoked*	*confirmed*
107th, 2002	*Lavenski R. Smith*	*Circuit Judge*	*1*	*invoked*	*confirmed*
107th, 2002	*Richard R. Clifton*	*Circuit Judge*	*1*	*invoked*	*confirmed*
107th, 2002	Richard H. Carmona	Surgeon General	1	invoked	confirmed
107th, 2002	*Julia Smith Gibbons*	*Circuit Judge*	*1*	*invoked*	*confirmed*

Table 4. (Continued)

Congress and Year	Nominee	Position	Number of Cloture Attempts[a]	Final Outcome of Cloture Attempt	Disposition of Nomination
107th, 2002	*Dennis W. Shedd*	*Circuit Judge*	*1*	*vitiated[x]*	*confirmed*
108th, 2003	*Victor J. Wolski*	*Judge, Court of Claims*	*1*	*vitiated*	*confirmed*
108th, 2003	*Miguel A. Estrada*	*Circuit Judge*	*7*	*rejected*	***withdrawn***
108th, 2003	Michael O. Leavitt	Administrator, Environmental Protection Agency	1	withdrawn	confirmed
108th, 2003	*Charles W. Pickering, Sr.*	*Circuit Judge*	*1*	***rejected***	***no final vote***
108th, 2003	*William H. Pryor, Jr.*	*Circuit Judge*	*2*	***rejected***	***no final vote***
108th, 2003	*Priscilla Richman Owen*	*Circuit Judge*	*4*	***rejected***	***no final vote***
108th, 2003	*Carolyn B. Kuhl*	*Circuit Judge*	*2*	***rejected***	***no final vote***
108th, 2003	*Janice R. Brown*	*Circuit Judge*	*1*	***rejected***	***no final vote***
108th, 2003	Thomas C. Dorr	Undersecretary of Agriculture for Rural Development and Board Member, Commodity[d] Credit Corporation	2	**rejected**	**no final vote**
108th, 2004	*Marcia G. Cooke*	*District Judge*	*1*	*withdrawn*	*confirmed*
108th, 2004	*William Gerry Myers III*	*Circuit Judge*	*1*	***rejected***	***no final vote***
108th, 2004	*David W. McKeague*	*Circuit Judge*	*1*	***rejected***	***no final vote***
108th, 2004	*Henry W. Saad*	*Circuit Judge*	*1*	***rejected***	***no final vote***
108th, 2004	*Richard A. Griffin*	*Circuit Judge*	*1*	***rejected***	***no final vote***

Table 4. (Continued)

Congress and Year	Nominee	Position	Number of Cloture Attempts[a]	Final Outcome of Cloture Attempt	Disposition of Nomination
109th, 2005	*Thomas C. Dorr*	Undersecretary of Agriculture for Rural Development	1	withdrawn	confirmed
109th, 2005	Peter Cyril Wyche Flory	Assistant Secretary ofDefense	1	**rejected**	**no final vote**
109th, 2005	*Priscilla Rich-man Owen*	*Circuit Court*	*1*	*invoked*	*confirmed*
109th, 2005	*William H. Pryor, Jr.*	*Circuit Court*	*1*	*invoked*	*confirmed*
109th, 2005	*Janice R. Brown*	*Circuit Judge*	*1*	*invoked*	*confirmed*
109th, 2005	John R. Bolton	U.S. Representative to the United Nations	2	rejected	**no final vote**
109th, 2005	Stephen L. Johnson	Administrator, Environmental ProtectionAgency	1	invoked	confirmed
109th, 2005	Robert J. Portman	U.S. Trade Representative	1	vitiated	confirmed
109th, 2006	Gordon England	Deputy Secretary of Defense	1	withdrawn	confirmed
109th, 2006	Eric S. Edelman	Under Secretary of Defense for Policy	1	withdrawn	confirmed
109th, 2006	Benjamin A. Powell	General Counsel, Office of the Director of National Intelligence	1	withdrawn	confirmed
109th, 2006	Richard Stickler	Assistant Secretary of Labor for Mine Safety and Health	1	withdrawn	**no final vote**

Table 4. (Continued)

Congress and Year	Nominee	Position	Number of Cloture Attempts[a]	Final Outcome of Cloture Attempt	Disposition of Nomination
109th, 2006	Dorrance Smith	Assistant Secretary of Defense	1	withdrawn	confirmed
109th, 2006	*Samuel A. Alito, Jr.*	*Associate Justice, Supreme Court*	*1*	*invoked*	*confirmed*
109th, 2006	*Brett M. Kavanaugh*	*Circuit Court*	*1*	*invoked*	*confirmed*
109th, 2006	Andrew von Eschenbach	Commissioner, Food and Drug Administration	1	invoked	confirmed
109th, 2006	Dirk Kempthorne	Secretary of the Interior	1	invoked	confirmed
109th, 2006	*Kent A. Jordan*	*Circuit Judge*	*1*	*invoked*	*confirmed*
110th, 2007	*Leslie Southwick*	*Circuit Judge*	*1*	*invoked*	*confirmed*

Sources: Compilations by CRS and Senate Library; Legislative Information System of the U.S. Congress; U.S. Congress, Senate, Committee on Rules and Administration, Senate Cloture Rule, committee print 99-95, 99th Congress, 1st session (Washington: GPO, 1985), pp. 44-70, 78-85; Congressional Record (Daily Digest); and Congressional Quarterly Almanac for 1986, 1987, 1992, 1995, 1999.

Notes: Executive branch nominations in roman; Judicial nominations in italic. Final outcome of cloture attempt is in bold when cloture was rejected. Disposition of nomination is in bold when the nominee was not confirmed.

a. Category includes both cloture motions filed and votes of the Senate to reconsider a cloture vote.

b. These five nominations to various positions in the State Department received consideration and cloture action concurrently, and are counted as one case in the table.

c. Cloture motion became moot and received no action.

d. The individual was nominated simultaneously for the two positions specified, and cloture action took place on each nomination in turn. The table counts all actions on one nominee as one case.

e. By unanimous consent, the Senate treated the cloture motion as having no effect.

POSITIONS IN RELATION TO WHICH CLOTURE WAS SOUGHT

Few of the nominations on which cloture has been attempted have been to the Supreme Court or Cabinet-level positions. Only four have been to the Supreme Court, and five to offices at the level of the President's Cabinet. In general, most nominations on which cloture has been sought have been to positions on the federal bench. This circumstance perhaps reflects the Senate's traditional inclination to permit the President generally wide latitude in selecting officials to serve under him in executive branch positions. Only in the 103rd and 109th Congresses was cloture sought chiefly on nominations to positions in the executive branch.

Of the 12 nominations on which cloture action occurred during the 103rd Congress, 10 were for executive branch positions. Of the 19 nominations on which cloture was sought in the 109th Congress, 12 were for executive branch positions. Except these Congresses, most nominations on which cloture has been sought have been to the federal courts. Table 3 summarizes the outcomes of cloture action on executive and judicial nominations, broken down into six periods that display distinct patterns.

End Notes

[1] Senate Rule XXII, paragraph 2. U.S. Senate, Committee on Rules and Administration, *Senate Manual, Containing the Standing Rules, Orders, Laws, and Resolutions Affecting the Business of the United States Senate*, S.Doc. 110-1, 100th Cong., 2nd sess., prepared by Matthew McGowan under the direction of Howard Gantman, Staff Director (Washington: GPO, 2009), sec. 22.2. During the 30 hours, no single Senator, other than the party floor leaders and the managers of the debate, may occupy more than one hour in debate.

[2] These questions of method are discussed in more detail in Richard S. Beth, "What We Don't Know About Filibusters," paper presented at the annual meeting of the Western Political Science Association, Portland, Ore., March 1995 (available from the author).

[3] U.S. Congress, Senate, Committee on Rules and Administration, *Senate Cloture Rule: Limitation of Debate in the Congress of the United States and Legislative History of Paragraph 2 of Rule XXII of the Standing Rules of the United States Senate (Cloture Rule)*, S.Print 99-95, prepared by the Congressional Research Service, Library of Congress, 99th Cong., 1st sess. (Washington: GPO, 1985), pp. 17, 21, 38-39, 105-112.

[4] For these purposes, five State Department nominations considered concurrently are counted as one, and each instance in which a single individual was simultaneously nominated to two positions is counted as one.

[5] The data include all cloture action in relation to a nomination, whether the motion is offered to close debate on the nominations itself or on a debatable motion to proceed to its consideration (which does not occur in practice after 1980).

[6] Committee on Rules and Administration, *Senate Cloture Rule*, pp. 30-32, 53-54, 119-121.

[7] The Republican Party lost control of the Senate during the 1st session of the 107th Congress. This analysis does not include the 111th Congress, in which the same party is in control of the Presidency, the Senate and the House.

In: Filibusters, Cloture and Holds in the Senate   ISBN: 978-1-61728-925-5
Editors: David J. Gilgram   © 2010 Nova Science Publishers, Inc.

Chapter 3

CLOTURE: ITS EFFECT ON SENATE PROCEEDINGS*

Walter J. Oleszek

Long known for its emphasis on lengthy deliberation, the Senate in most circumstances allows its Members to debate issues for as long as they want. Further, the Senate has few ways either to limit the duration of debates or to bring filibusters (extended "talkathons") to an end. For instance, a Senator may offer a non-debatable motion to table (or kill) an amendment or he or she might ask unanimous consent to restrict debate on pending matters. The Senate has one formal rule — Rule XXII — for imposing limits on the further consideration of an issue. Called the cloture rule (for closure of debate), Rule XXII became part of the Senate's rulebook in 1917 and has been amended several times since.

Under its current formulation, Rule XXII requires a cloture petition (signed by 16 Senators) to be presented to the Senate. Two days later, and one hour after the Senate convenes, the presiding officer is required to order a live quorum call (often waived by unanimous consent) and, after its completion, to put this question to the membership: "Is it the sense of the Senate that debate shall be brought to a close?" If three-fifths of the entire Senate membership (60 of 100) votes in the affirmative, cloture is invoked and the Senate is

---

* This is an edited, reformatted and augmented version of a CRS Report for Congress publication dated May 2008.

subject to post-cloture procedures that will eventually end the debate and bring the clotured question (a bill, amendment, or motion, for example) to a vote. (To end debate on a measure or motion to amend Senate rules requires approval by two-thirds of the Senators present and voting.)

If cloture is invoked under the terms of Rule XXII, then Senate floor activity is thereafter subject to a variety of conditions and constraints. Several of the main post- cloture features include:

30-HOUR TIME CAP

Thirty hours of further consideration is permitted on the clotured question with time used for such things as roll-call votes or quorum calls charged against the 30-hour cap. As Senate precedents state, "the time used for roll call votes, quorum calls, reading of amendments, points of order and inquiries to and responses by the Chair, and the like, is charged against the 30 hours. Therefore, it is quite possible that the total debate by Senators could be far less than 30 hours." The 30-hour period may be extended if three-fifths of all Senators duly chosen and sworn agree to the increase.

ONE-HOUR OF DEBATE PER SENATOR

Under cloture, each Senator is entitled to an hour of debate on a "first come, first served" basis. Senators may yield all or portions of their one hour to a floor manager or a party leader but neither may be yielded more than two additional hours. "Any Senator may yield back to the Chair some or all of his 1 hourfor debate under cloture," say the precedents, "but such yielding would not reduce the total time available for consideration of the clotured matter."

PRE-FILING OF AMENDMENTS

Only amendments that have been filed before the cloture vote may be considered once cloture is invoked. First-degree amendments must be filed by 1:00 p.m. on the day after the filing of the cloture petition; second-degree amendments may be filed until at least one hour prior to the start of the cloture vote. As Rule XXII explains:

Except by unanimous consent, no amendment shall be proposed after the vote to bring the debate to a close, unless it had been submitted in writing to the Journal Clerk by 1 o'clock p.m. on the day following the filing of the cloture motion if an amendment in the first degree, and unless it had been so submitted at least one hour prior to the beginning of the cloture vote if an amendment in the second degree.

ROLE OF THE PRESIDING OFFICER

Under cloture, the presiding officer has authority that he or she does not have during regular Senate proceedings. For example, on his or her initiative, the presiding officer may rule out-of-order dilatory motions or amendments, including quorum calls. The chair also has the authority to count to determine the presence of a quorum. During regular Senate sessions, the chair is obligated under Senate Rule VI, if a Senator suggests the absence of a quorum, to "forthwith direct the Secretary to call the roll...."

NO NONGERMANE AMENDMENTS

The Senate does not have a general rule of germaneness for amendments. However, once cloture is invoked, all amendments (and debate) are to be germane to the clotured proposal. Senate precedents state that "the Chair may take the initiative and rule amendments out of order as not being germane without a point of order being made, and when obviously non-germane the Chair may rule the amendment out of order even before it has been read or stated by the clerk." Senate precedents add that under cloture "one of the tests of germaneness is whether the amendment limits or restricts the provisions contained in the bill. If it is clearly restrictive it would be held germane."

POINTS OF ORDER AND APPEALS NOT DEBATABLE

Rule XXII states that points of order, "including questions of relevancy, and appeals from the decision of the Presiding Officer, shall be decided without debate." Senate precedents make plain that the chair occasionally has held appeals to be dilatory, but precedents also underscore that "the right to appeal is a basic right of each Senator and would be held dilatory only in the most extraordinary circumstances." Worth noting is that on one occasion, in 1977, "the Chair denied a Senator the right to make a point of order."

THE UNFINISHED BUSINESS

The invocation of cloture on a measure or matter means, as stated in Rule XXII, that it "shall be the unfinished business to the exclusion of all other business until disposed of." Senate precedents buttress this point by adding that the "adoption of a cloture motion on a measure prohibits the consideration of any other business except that which is transacted by unanimous consent."

In: Filibusters, Cloture and Holds in the Senate   ISBN: 978-1-61728-925-5
Editors: David J. Gilgram   © 2010 Nova Science Publishers, Inc.

Chapter 4

"HOLDS" IN THE SENATE*

Walter J. Oleszek

SUMMARY

Holds are an informal device unique to the upper body. They permit a single Senator or any number of Senators to stop—sometimes temporarily, sometimes permanently—floor consideration of measures or matters that are available to be scheduled by the Senate. A hold, in brief, is a request by a Senator to his or her party leader to delay floor action on a measure or matter. It is up to the majority leader to decide whether, or for how long, he will honor a colleague's hold. Scheduling the business of the Senate is the fundamental prerogative of the majority leader, and it is done in consultation with the minority leader.

BACKGROUND

Relatively little is known about holds, and their exact origin appears lost in the mists of history. They probably evolved from the early traditions of comity, courtesy, reciprocity, and accommodation that characterized the

---

* This is an edited, reformatted and augmented version of a CRS Report for Congress publication dated May 2008.

Senate's work. Holds have received limited attention from scholars, journalists, or pundits, in part because there is hardly any public record of who places holds, how it is done (often by letter to the party leader), how many holds are placed on any bill, or how long they will be honored by the majority leadership. The list of Democratic and Republican Senators who have holds on various measures is kept by the respective leaders of each party.

Only Senators may use holds, but there have been instances when they have been invoked by legislative staff. House Members, lobbyists, or executive officials may request Senators to place holds on measures or matters that they prefer the Senate not take up. Originally used by Senators to ensure that they would be notified in advance about any time-limitation agreement or motion to proceed and consulted about certain bills and nominations that may be brought to the floor, holds have evolved to become a potent extra-parliamentary practice.

POTENCY OF HOLDS

Holds are a potent blocking device because they are linked to the Senate's tradition of extended debate and unanimous consent agreements. Party leaders understand that to ignore holds could precipitate objections to unanimous consent requests and filibusters. Unlike filibusters, which may be partly educational in their purpose and which are televised nationally over C-SPAN, holds require no public utterance. Little surprise that holds are sometimes referred to as a "silent filibuster."

Holds are useful devices for gaining leverage and fostering negotiations. Senators, for example, may indicate that they have holds on measures or nominations to alert appropriate colleagues that they want to be consulted about a measure or nomination, signal displeasure with the administration, or retaliate in kind against lawmakers who have placed holds on their bills. In today's workload-packed and deadline-driven Senate, holds are often particularly effective at the end of a session when sponsors of measures may be more open to compromise with the lawmakers having holds on their bills. Holds, too, have the virtue of giving lawmakers additional time to study legislation, especially during the end-of-session rush to adjourn, and alerting party leaders to potential scheduling problems.

TYPES OF HOLDS

Informally, there have been attempts by some analysts to classify holds. For example, there are so-called *informational* holds, where Senators wish to be informed or consulted before a measure or nomination is brought to the floor; *revolving* or *rotating* holds, where one Senator, and then another and so on, will place holds; *Mae West* holds, which suggest that the Senator(s) who employed the hold wants to bargain with the proponents of the legislation or nomination; *retaliatory*, or *tit-for-tat*, holds; and *choke* holds, where the objective is to kill the affected bill ornomination. The use of *secret* or *anonymous* holds has triggered the most recent proposals for reform.

CALLS FOR CHANGE

Over the years, Senators and party leaders have suggested that changes need to be made in the use of holds, see CRS Report RL31685, *Proposals to Reform "Holds" in the Senate*, by Walter J. Oleszek. The objective of the proposals is not to eliminate the practice but to subject it to openness and accountability. For example, in 2006 the Senate adopted an amendment to an ethics and lobbying bill (S. 2349) requiring Senators who place holds on measures or matters to publish that fact in the *Congressional Record* within three days after they have provided written notice to a party leader. S. 2349 failed to be enacted into law. The next year the Senate adopted—for the first time ever—a formal and statutory policy limiting the ability of Senators to place anonymous holds with the enactment into law of S. 1, the Honest Leadership and Open Government Act (P.L. 110-81). The new holds policy is outlined in Section 512 of S. 1, and is titled "Notice of Objecting to Proceeding." Section 512 lays out the exact steps for making a secret hold public,see CRS Report RL34255, *Senate Policy on "Holds": Action in the 110th Congress*, by Walter J. Oleszek. The newness of Section 512 means that it remains a work in progress. Some time needs to pass before an assessment might be made of its impact and influence on senatorial decision- making and behavior.

In: Filibusters, Cloture and Holds in the Senate   ISBN: 978-1-61728-925-5
Editors: David J. Gilgram   © 2010 Nova Science Publishers, Inc.

Chapter 5

SENATE POLICY ON "HOLDS": ACTION IN THE 110TH CONGRESS*

Walter J. Oleszek

SUMMARY

When the Honest Leadership and Open Government Act (S. 1, 110th Congress) was signed into law on September 14, 2007, Section 512 of that statute specifically addressed the issue of secret "holds." Holds are a longstanding custom of the Senate that enabled Members to provide notice to their party leader of their intent to object on the floor to taking up or passing a measure or matter. Their potency as a blocking, delaying, or bargaining device is linked to Senators' ability to conduct filibusters or object to unanimous consent agreements or requests. The new holds process outlined in Section 512 is designed to constrain the frequency of anonymous holds and promote more openness and transparency with respect to their use. Ultimately, it is up to the majority leader of the Senate—who sets the chamber's agenda after consulting various people—to decide whether, or for how long, he will honor a colleague's hold.

---

* This is an edited, reformatted and augmented version of a CRS Report for Congress publication dated March 2008.

INTRODUCTION

On September 14, 2007, President George W. Bush signed into law the Honest Leadership and Open Government Act (S. 1, 110th Congress). The bill addressed a wide variety of topics such as ethics, campaign finance, and lobbying. S. 1 also made a number of procedural revisions affecting the Senate, one which is the focus of this chapter. Section 512 of Title V of the new law (P.L. 110- 81) specifically dealt with the issue of "holds." Holds are an informal custom of the Senate that, until enactment of S. 1, were mentioned neither in chamber rules or precedents nor in any statute. A hold, as one Senator explained, is "a notice by a Senator to his or her party leader of an intention to object to bringing a bill or nomination to the floor for consideration."[1] Their potency as a blocking, delaying, or bargaining device is linked to Senators' ability to conduct filibusters or object to unanimous consent agreements or requests. To be sure, it is ultimately up to the majority leader of the Senate—who sets the chamber's agenda after consulting various people—to decide whether, or for how long, he will honor a colleague's hold. If the majority leader cannot get unanimous consent to bring up a measure or matter, then he can make a motion to call it up. That motion is subject to extended debate, but no Senator can, under the practices of the Senate, prevent the majority leader from making that motion.

The controversy that precipitated enactment of Section 512 involved secret or anonymous holds. Two Senators in particular worked for years to end the practice of lawmakers placing secret holds on measures or matters. Their goal was not to eliminate holds but to infuse the custom with transparency and accountability so Senators would know which of their colleagues had holds on various bills or nominations. Knowing which Senator(s) has a hold on a measure or matter enables senatorial advocates of those proposals to meet with the "holder" to discuss whether, or under what circumstances, the hold might be lifted.

In 2006, for example, these two proponents of ending secret holds succeeded in winning adoption of an amendment to an ethics, lobbying, and rules reform package (S. 2349) that would end the practice by establishing a new standing order of the Senate. Like Section 512 of S. 1, their amendment required the majority and minority leaders to recognize a hold—called a "notice of intent to object to proceeding"—only if it was provided in writing by a Member of their caucus. Moreover, noted a former party leader, "for the hold to be honored, the Senator objecting would have to publish his objection in the *Congressional Record* 3 days after the notice is provided to a leader."[2] One of the principal authors of the amendment provided this explanation of their proposal:

> Our proposed standing order would provide that a simple form be filled out, much like we do when we add co-sponsors to a bill. Senators would have a full 3 session days from placing the hold to submit the form [to their respective party leader]. The hold would then be published in the CONGRESSIONAL RECORD and the Senate Calendar. It is just as simple as that.[3]

Nothing in the author's amendment required the majority leader to honor a formal notice of intent to object to proceeding (or hold) or any other "message" by a Member that he or she intends to oppose any unanimous consent request to take up a measure or matter. S. 2349 required enactment into law before the new holds policy could take effect, but the 109th Congress adjourned before this could occur. With the passage of S. 1 in 2007, the Senate adopted—for the first time ever—a formal and statutory policy limiting the ability of Senators to place anonymous holds.

LIMITS ON SECRET HOLDS: THE NEW POLICY

The new holds policy in Section 512 is titled "Notice of Objecting to Proceeding." Its fundamental purpose is to promote more openness and transparency in the holds process. Section 512 is neither a Senate rules change nor a standing order of the Senate, except as to the establishment of "notice of intent" calendars by the Secretary of the Senate. Instead, Section 512 is directive to the majority and minority leaders of the Senate stating that before a hold is recognized by them, certain procedures must be observed by Senators. In effect, it is the responsibility of each Member to comply with the terms of the new policy. There is no enforcement device or method to ensure compliance, except the stipulation that party leaders shall not honor a "notice of intent" (or hold) if Senators do not follow the specified procedures. (The majority and minority leaders consult regularly about the Senate's agenda, and keep each other apprised of Members who have placed holds on measures or matters.) Section 512 states:

(a) In general—The Majority Leaders and Minority Leaders of the Senate or their designees shall recognize a notice of intent of a Senator who is a member of their caucus to object to proceeding to a measure or matter only if the Senator—

(1) following the objection to a unanimous consent to proceeding to, and, or passage of, a measure or matter on their behalf, submits the notice of intent in writing to the appropriate leader or their designee; and

(2) not later than 6 session days after the submission under paragraph (1), submits for inclusion in the Congressional Record and in the applicable calendar section described in subsection (b) the following notice:

'I, Senator XXXX, intend to object to proceedings to XXXX, dated XXXX for the following reasons XXXX.'

(b) Calendar—

(1) IN GENERAL—The Secretary of the Senate shall establish for both the Senate Calendar of Business and the Senate Executive Calendar a separate section entitled 'Notice of Intent to Object to Proceeding'.

(2) CONTENT—The section required by paragraph (1) shall include—

(A) the name of each Senator filing a notice under subsection (a)(2);

(B) the measure or matter covered by the calendar that the Senator objects to; and

(C) the date the objection was filed.

(3) NOTICE—A Senator who has notified their respective leader and who has withdrawn their objection within the 6 session day period is not required to submit a notification under subsection (a)(2).

(c) Removal—A Senator may have an item with respect to the Senator removed from a calendar to which it was added under subsection (b) by submitting for inclusion in the Congressional Record the following notice:

'I, Senator XXXX, do not object to proceed to XXXX, dated XXXX.'

To summarize, the formal process to curb secret holds is triggered when certain steps are followed by a Senator. These steps apply in limited circumstances and could be bypassed in at least two ways: (1) if Senators, on their own initiative, publicly state that they have holds on measures or matters or, alternatively, they simply object on their own to a unanimous consent request to call up a measure or matter; or (2) they privately inform their party leader of their intent to block floor consideration of certain measures or matters, and the majority leader never requests that they come up. As a Senator stated, the "mere threat of a hold prevents unanimous consent requests [to take up measures or matters] from being made in the first place."[4] The principal features of Section 512 specify the exact steps for making a secret hold public.

- The process begins when any Senator states that he or she, on behalf of a colleague, is objecting to a unanimous consent request—commonly made by the majority leader or the majority floor manager—to proceed to or pass a measure or matter.
- That colleague must then submit a notice of intent (a hold) letter to the appropriate party leader (or their designee) specifying the reason(s) for his or her objection(s) to a certain measure or matter.
- Not later than six session days after submission of the "notice of intent" letter, the Senator placing the hold submits the notice to be printed in the *Congressional Record* and in a separate section of the appropriate calendar.
- The majority leader and the minority leader (or their respective designee) are then obliged to recognize a hold placed by a Member of their caucus. ("Recognition" does not mean that the majority leader—who schedules the Senate's business—must honor the hold.)
- A Senator may withdraw his or her hold prior to the expiration of the 6-sessionday period. He or she is then under no obligation to have their hold letter printed in the *Congressional Record* and noted in the appropriate Senate calendar.
- To remove their hold from the appropriate Senate calendar, a Senator submits a notice for inclusion in the *Congressional Record* stating that he or she no longer objects to proceeding to a measure or matter.

Worth underscoring is that under the terms of Section 512, a Senator is required to disclose his or her hold only after another lawmaker formally objects on their behalf to a unanimous consent request to proceed to a measure or matter. If the Senator who is the "true" objector wants to continue with the Section 512 process, he or she must then submit a notice of intent leader to their party leader. Then the six-session-day clock begins to tick. (Just when the six-session-day period starts and ends may require specific parameters.) Until an objection is made on the floor of the Senate, a secret hold could exist for days, weeks, or months without any knowledge of that reality by the sponsors and advocates of bills or nominations.

It is also useful to note that a Senator who publicly objects on his or her own behalf to a unanimous consent request to proceed to or pass a measure need not follow the Section 512 process. The disclosure has occurred publicly and Members know who is the objector. Thus, the name of the objector would not be required to be published in the *Congressional Record* or the appropriate calendar of the Senate.

Several reasons account for the six-day lapse before Senators are obliged to transmit a notice of intent letter to their party leader. The six days gives Members time to study a measure or matter; receive feedback from affected state agencies, if any; or, if necessary, draft an amendment to a measure that addresses their specific concerns. For example, on bills that are "hotlined"—special telephone lines in Members' offices to inform them of the two party leaders' intent to pass legislation by unanimous consent unless lawmakers object within a certain time period—Senators might take exception to a bill's prompt consideration on the floor because they want several days to review the measure. The six days enable Senators to research and decide what their reaction to a measure should be without being criticized for delaying action on a bill or subjected to outside special interest pressure for having a hold on a group-backed bill when the end result might be senatorial approval of the legislation.

Furthermore, although Section 512's goal, as already noted, is to promote more openness in the holds process, Senators have numerous private ways to inform party leaders of their opposition to measures or matters. These types of private "messages"—personal letters, telephone calls, hallway chats, e-mails, and so on—could be characterized as the functional equivalent of secret holds. If the majority leader is out "running on the National Mall [and] another senator comes running by and shouts as he passes, 'I'm going to block that bill.' Is that a hold? Senators are always going to find a way to signal their concerns to the leadership," noted a legislative scholar.[5] A recent example occurred at the start of the 110th Congress when a Senator on February 5, 2007, sent a "Dear Colleague" letter to all Members. The letter's purpose was to communicate to all Senators "a list of principles I will use to evaluate new legislation in the 110th Congress. I also want to give you advance notice I intend to object to consideration of legislation that violates these common sense principles."[6]

The newness of Section 512 means that there is not yet much information or evidence of how the policy for limiting secret holds is to be implemented in practice. As one of the Senate's principal advocates for ending anonymous holds said shortly after S. 1 was signed into law, "I have to tell my colleagues that I don't know how [Section 512] is going to work."[7] A section-by-section analysis of S. 1 was inserted in the *Congressional Record* by the relevant committee chair to provide some legislative history regarding the procedures for constraining secret holds.[8] Time, experience, and ongoing parliamentary familiarity with the new procedures seem likely to answer various questions that surely will arise as to Section 512's practical application. Among several questions or issues about Section 512 that might require answers are the following, mentioned in no special order of priority.

SECTION 512: SELECTED ISSUES

Retroactive Application

Will the new statutory policy apply retroactively to holds placed on measures or matters prior to S. 1 's enactment into law? A recent bill sets this question in bold relief. A measure to require Senators to file their campaign finance reports electronically has been the subject of a hold at least since March 2007, according to press accounts. As a journalist reported, "For months, liberal bloggers and activists have been agitating to unmask the mystery senator who has been blocking action, by means of a secret 'hold,' on a key campaign finance disclosure bill. Now they may finally get their wish [with enactment into law of S. 1]."[9]

When a unanimous consent request was made on September 24, 2007, to take up the bill (S. 223) requiring the electronic filing of campaign finance reports, a Senator objected. Yet it was not clear whether the Senator in fact had placed a secret hold on the bill.[10] (To be sure, the Senator might have previously and privately informed party leaders that he would object to calling up S. 223.) The Senator's staff denied that the Member had an anonymous hold on the bill, and GOP leadership aides stated that Republican objections to the bill did not "amount to a 'hold'."[11] On the other hand, one Senator stated that the Member who objected publicly "has made it plain that he is the one holding up the bill by insisting on offering an unrelated amendment" requiring outside organizations that file ethics complaints against Senators to list donors who have contributed $5,000 or more to the organization.[12] Another Senator, citing Section 512's immediate applicability to Senate proceedings, said in six legislative days "we must know who it is" who placed the hold on S. 223.[13] (Section 512 became effective when the President signed S. 1 into law.)

Three days later, on September 27, the same Senator who objected to bringing up S. 223 asked unanimous consent to call up that bill but with the stipulation that only his aforementioned amendment would be made in orderfor floor consideration. He observed that "there are anonymous outside groups who are filing ethics complaints" for political reasons and the Senate needs "to know that" and transparency is "the best way to find that out."[14] A Senator objected to that request on behalf of the chair of the reporting committee. Then, in a first for the Senate, Section 512 was formally invoked when the chair of the relevant committee of jurisdiction sent a letter to the majority leader. The letter stated in part:

As you know, under the provisions of the Honest Leadership and Open Government Act of 2007 (section 512 of P.L. 110-81), a Senator is required to submit a "Notice of Intent to Object" letter when another Senator objects to a unanimous consent request on his/her behalf. Please consider this letter as my notice of intent to object ... [to a colleague's] proposed [non-germane] amendment to S. 223, the Senate Campaign Disclosure Parity Act.... [15]

As required by Section 512, the letter identified the Senator placing the hold, the date the objection was filed, and the reason(s) for objecting to proceeding to a measure or matter. The Senator's letter was printed in a new "Notice of Intent" section of the *Congressional Record*. Subsequently, the *Calendar of Business* of the Senate included the Senator's objection in the required section entitled "Notice of Intent to Object to Proceeding." Recall that Section 512 calls upon the Secretary of the Senate to establish such a section in both the *Calendar of Business* and the *Executive Calendar*. Since enactment of Section 512, no Senator has come forward to state affirmatively and explicitly that he or she has a hold on S. 223.[16] Moreover, it is not clear if other Senators have indicated to their respective party leader that they would object to calling up the campaign bill.

Under the terms of Section 512, and this point is made in the above-cited letter, a Senator is required to disclose his or her hold only after another lawmaker—on behalf of a fellow colleague—objects to a unanimous consent request to proceed. Then the six-session-day clock begins to tick. (Just when the six-session-day period starts and ends may require additional clarification.) Until an objection is made, a secret hold could exist for days, weeks, or months without any knowledge of that reality by the sponsors and advocates of bills or nominations. To be sure, Senators can publicly announce their holds in whatever way or forum they prefer.[17] Some Senators have a policy of always publicly announcing their holds.

Scope of Coverage

Section 512 addresses measures or matters. Past practices regarding the placement of holds on measures or matters appear likely to continue in effect, but this issue might give rise to questions that require clarification. The Senate's tradition of holds has long been an informal practice, so there is relatively little detailed public information about this custom. For example, there is no official public Senate record of who places holds; how many holds are placed by Senators on different types of bills, nominations, or other matters; how long holds are honored by the majority leader; the differences among hold requests; the frequency of holds during different periods of a legislative session; or which Senators are more or less likely to place holds, such as majority or minority lawmakers, senior rather than junior Senators, or liberal versus conservative Members.

Available public materials on the custom appear to suggest that holds may be placed on various types of measures or matters—although there is no definitive list, so far as is known, of the various measures and matters that over time have been the subject of holds. Party records are likely to be incomplete and lack important information. "Hold" letters may also be housed in the personal papers or archives of former party leaders.[18]

A Senator may remove a hold at any time, and Section 512 specifies the procedure for removing a public hold from the Senate's two calendars. The lifting of a hold by a Member does not prevent other Senators from putting holds on the same measure or nomination.

With Section 512's adoption, it is not certain whether some or all of the past practices on holds will still be observed. Whether these past practices are fully known is not clear because of, as mentioned, the traditional secrecy surrounding the practice. For example, extant public information on holds indicates that they have been placed on certain privileged business, such as conference reports.[19] In 2002, for instance, it was reported that a Senator had placed a secret hold on a Justice Department authorization conference report.[20] If Section 512 applies to conference reports, can holds also be placed on a related bicameral matter: amendments between the chambers, which are also privileged matters? Holds on privileged business seem less likely to be honored, or honored for any lengthy period, because the motion to take them up is non-debatable.

Unclear, too, is whether the new policy on holds would continue to apply to various non- privileged business, such as the selection of conferees. As former Senator William S. Cohen, R- Me., wrote, "I wanted to be appointed a conferee ... and [Armed Services] Chairman [John] Stennis was unlikely to add my name to the list if I made such a request. I put a 'hold' on the naming of conferees ... , which upset Chairman Stennis."[21] Secret holds have made it difficult at times for the Senate to agree to the usually routine motion to go to conference with the House to iron out bicameral disagreements on legislation: "Mr. President, I move that the Senate insist on its amendments [or disagree to the House amendments], request a conference with the House on the disagreeing votes thereon, and that the Chair be authorized to appoint conferees." Any Senator can object to this unanimous consent request, and the floor manager would then have to make three separate motions (insist or disagree, request, and authorize). Each motion is subject to a filibuster, noted a former Senate parliamentarian, and require "three separate cloture votes to close debate, and that takes a lot of time. It basically stops the whole process of going to conference."[22] In 2007, on a bill (S. 378) to improve court security, a proponent of the measure stated that "we are being blocked from going to conference" by an anonymous hold.[23]

Three Other Possible Issues

First, a topic that might require additional clarity is whether holds can still be applied to a class of related measures or matters. Recall that the language of Section 512 requires the following notice: "I, Senator XXXX, intend to object to proceedings to XXXX.... " Accordingly, would it still be possible for a Senator to place a hold on all judicial nominations or treaties pending on the Executive Calendar, or on all measures on the General Orders Calendar dealing with a specific topic reported by one of the standing committees? Or is it the intent of Section 512 to require Senators to disclose their reasons as to why they are objecting for each measure or matter?

Second, the majority leader, as noted earlier, is the "decider" when it comes to honoring holds. Often, the majority leader will honor holds, at least for a period of time, both as a courtesy to colleagues and as recognition that ignoring a hold could trigger time-consuming dilatory tactics in an institution that is typically workload packed and deadline -driven. On the other hand, if the majority leader places holds on his own behalf—on pending judicial nominations, for example— there are few, if any, effective ways to override the majority leader's decision. How, too, are Members to know if the majority leader has anonymous holds on measures or matters if he does not ask unanimous consent to call them up? Furthermore, if a Senator placing a hold is a member of the majority party, the majority leader might not even ask unanimous consent of the Senate to take up a measure or matter. The result: no public disclosure of which Senator has a hold on the bill. As a Senator said:

> For instance, it is not clear to me what would happen if the minority leader asked unanimous consent to proceed to a bill and the majority leader objected on his own behalf to protect his prerogative to set the agenda but also having the effect of honoring the hold of another member of the majority leader's caucus. Or what if the majority leader asked unanimous consent to proceed to a bill and the minority leader objects but does not specify on whose behalf, even though a member of the minority party has a hold. Would the minority Senator with the hold then be required to disclose the hold? I don't know. It is not very clear.[24]

Third, Section 512, as already mentioned, obligates Senators to specify their reasons for objecting to consideration of a measure or matter in a notice of intent (a hold) letter sent to their party's leader. Multiple reasons influence why Senators might place a hold on a bill or nomination. Sometimes a hold is employed to achieve purposes completely unrelated to action on the specific bill or nominee. Senators may place holds on bills or nominees they support because they want to gain bargaining "leverage" on an unrelated matter with the Administration, a colleague, a committee chair, or the other chamber. As one Senator told a colleague who asked why he had placed a hold on his bill:

> I have no objection to your bill at all, Senator, but another Senator who chairs a committee has a hold on one of my bills, and, therefore, I looked up and down the list to see what bills were under his jurisdiction and I found yours. And so I put a hold on the bill reported out of committee.[25]

A Senate party leader remarked that there have been times when holds have been applied to "every piece of a committee's legislation ... by an individual or group of senators, not because they wish to be involved in consideration of those bills, but as a means of achieving unrelated purposes or leverage."[26]

Senators might use a "retaliatory hold" against Members who are blocking floor consideration of their preferred legislation. Senators might be requested to place holds by House members, executive officials, or lobbyists. In specifying why they are placing holds per the instructions contained in Section 512, are Senators expected to have complete discretion as to how many reasons and how much detail they provide in their notice-of-intent letters? Or might the two party leaders expect a reasonable amount of pertinent information—either stated in the notice of intent letter or through other non-public ways—on which they can make or evaluate their scheduling decisions?

CONCLUDING OBSERVATIONS

Section 512 is a work in progress. Some time needs to pass before a reasonable assessment can be made of its impact and influence on senatorial decision-making and behavior. Experience in implementing Section 512 will no doubt provide clarity and perspective as to how the new provision is working in practice and whether it is fulfilling its fundamental purpose: to infuse greater transparency in the holds process. Like any new change, Section 512 might also have unforeseen consequences. For example, holds do not have to be made public for six Senate session days following an objection to proceeding to a measure or matter. One implication is that there might be a surge of secret holds during the final few days of a legislative session, "more than enough time to effectively kill a bill or nominee in complete secrecy," said a Senator.[27]

Senators might organize a "revolving" hold. Once an objection under Section 512 is made to a unanimous consent request, then one Member, then another, and so on might place a hold on a measure or matter but then remove it prior to the expiration of the six-session-day period. (Each lawmaker would still need to file a notice of intent letter with their party's leader.) Simply the possibility that one or more Senators appear willing to stall action on a measure or matter might dissuade the majority leader from even trying to proceed to a bill or nomination. Under this parliamentary scenario, none of the Senators who oppose a bill or nomination would have to publicly disclose that they had a hold on the measure or matter. (It is also unclear whether an individual Senator—prior to the end of the six-session-day period—could lift his or her hold and then reimpose it repeatedly following a colleague's objection on his or her behalf to a unanimous consent request made pursuant to the provisions of Section 512).

Section 512 also might promote greater use of public holds. Outside special interests, for example, might encourage Senators to use the new holds process to demonstrate their support for the group's agenda priorities. In the judgment of one congressional scholar, "We could easily imagine different interest groups seeking out senators to go public with objections and say, 'This is an opportunity for you to highlight an issue that's important to our constituency.'"[28] Senators, in short, may welcome the chance to admit and trumpet to the press, media, and their constituents that they have a hold on certain measures or matters. The hold, as political scientists would say, could be a form of position-taking and credit-claiming that might enhance Senators' re-election prospects.

On the other hand, Section 512 might produce a decline in the use of holds. "I assume people will think twice before it is publicly distributed that they are stopping legislation," remarked a former Senate parliamentarian.[29] A Senator did not see it this way, however. "If I don't agree with [a bill], why am I going to let it go?" he asked. The members think [Section 512] will intimidate people into not holding bills, but it doesn't bother me."[30] Needless to say, to make an assessment of whether public holds might increase or decline given the enactment of Section 512 is problematic because of its limited applicability. Senators have a wide array of techniques—which are akin to secret holds—to inform party leaders of their intent to block action on measures or matters. Senators, too, have always been able to make their holds public.

To conclude, over the years, various Senators and party leaders have tried different ways to infuse more accountability and uniformity in the use of holds and to make clear that they are not a veto on the majority leader's prerogative of proposing measures or matters for Senate consideration.[31] Party leaders understand that holds function as an "early warning system" by alerting them to potential problems in scheduling measures or matters. They also recognize that holds are less than sacrosanct as legislative circumstances change, such as the approach of deadlines or the need to enact "must pass" legislation. Still, it goes without saying that holds are a prominent feature of the contemporary Senate. Members realize their political and policy potential both as a form of "silent filibuster" and as a bargaining device. Holds influence the lawmaking and confirmation processes, and the statutory policy seems certain to shed additional light on this heretofore largely behind-the-scenes custom. As a key proponent of ending secret holds said about Section 512, "It's a start."[32]

End Notes

[1] *Congressional Record*, vol. 148, April 17, 2002, p. S2850. Two other views of holds are provided by a former Senate Majority Leader and a Republican Senator As the majority

leader stated: "In many instances, Senators put holds on a bill, not to prevent its coming up, but to alert the respective party floor staffs, that they want to be notified before the bill is called up. They may have amendments. They may want to be notified when it is coming up. So it is not always for the purpose of keeping a bill from coming up." See *Congressional Record*, vol. 133, December 9, 1987, p. 34449. The GOP Senator said: A hold is "a notice that a Senator wishes to be on the floor when the matter which is the subject of his interest is considered so he might protect his rights." He added: Within reason, it means that "my leader, or the floor manager or whomever is responsible, is obligated by the traditions and customs of this body to call me up on the telephone and say, 'You better get over here if you want to be protected. If you are going to exercise your hold, that means come over here and object or come over and debate the motion.' It happens thousands of times a year." See *Congressional Record*, vol. 132, February 20, 1986, p. S1465.

2 *Congressional Record*, vol. 152, March 28, 2006, p. S2458.

3 Ibid., March 8, 2006, p. S1874. During a colloquy on the proposal, a Senator asked for a clarification of the amendment's intent with respect to what she called a "temporary hold." She stated: "Let me give you a specific example. Occasionally, bills will be discharged from their authorizing committees. These are not necessarily on the calendar. They are discharged from the committee, and the bill will be hotlined on both of our sides to see if there is any objection. Obviously, putting a temporary stay on the consideration of a discharged bill in order to allow a few hours for review or even a day for review is completely different from the practice of secretly killing a bill by putting an indefinite anonymous hold." In response, one of the main authors of the amendment agreed with the Senator, and remarked that "we make very clear that it is not our intention to bar those consults. We like to use the word 'consult,' which is a protected tool for a Senator as opposed to the question of a hold. I think perhaps another way to clarify it is a consult is sort of like a yellow light. You put up a little bit of caution—that we need a bit of time to take a look at it. A hold is a red light when you are not supposed to go forward. We don't want people to be able to exercise those holds in secret.... In fact, to ensure that we have this kind of [consult] procedure ... , we call for 3 days before an individual has to put in the CONGRESSIONAL RECORD that they have a hold on a matter." Ibid., p. S1874.

4 *Congressional Record*, vol. 153, September 19, 2007, p. S11743.

5 Brian Friel, "Wrestling With Holds," *National Journal*, January 13, 2007, p. 47.

6 The letter is available from the author of this chapter.

7 *Congressional Record*, vol. 153, September 19, 2007, p. S1 1742.

8 Ibid., August 2, 2007, p. S10711.

9 Eliza Newlin Carney, "No Hiding Place," *National Journal*, September 22, 2007, Inside Washington.

10 Emily Pierce, "Mystery Still Surrounds Filing Hold," *Roll Call*, September 26, 2007, p. 1.

11 Ibid., p. 17.

12 *Congressional Record*, vol. 153, September 24, 2007, p. S1 1998.

13 Ibid., p. S11997.

14 *Congressional Record*, vol. 153, September 27, 2007, p. S12207.

15 *Congressional Record*, vol. 153, October 2, 2007, p. S12419. This notice of intent letter was inserted in the *Congressional Record* by the majority leader. The next day the author of the letter also placed it in the *Congressional Record*, p. S12561.

16 It might be worth noting that Section 512 specifically references holds placed by a Senator. It does not address the case of a group of Senators who object to proceeding to a measure or matter. If the willingness to block a measure or matter is the collective decision of an informal or formal group Members, there might be uncertainty as to which group member is expected to transmit a "notice of intent" letter to their party leader. In such a case, it seems likely that the relevant party leader would lodge an objection on behalf of a number of Members who oppose the legislation or nomination. The leader's objection on behalf of a

group of Members would not appear to initiate the provisions of Section 512, which focus on "a Senator."

[17] See, for example, Tim Starks, "Senate Panel OKs Surveillance Bill," *CQ Today*, October 19, 2007, p. 1.

[18] See an unpublished paper by C. Lawrence Evans and Daniel Lipinski, "Holds, Legislation, and the Senate Parties," April 2005. This chapter analyzed almost 1,000 holds found in the personal papers of former Senate Majority Leader Howard Baker, TN. The author has a copy of the Evans-Lipinski paper and will make it available upon request.

[19] For a list of privileged measures or matters, see Floyd M. Riddick and Alan S. Frumin, *Senate Procedure: Precedents and Practices* (Washington: GPO, 1992), pp. 1034-1035.

[20] Jennifer A. Diouhy, "Justice Department Authorization Signals 'New Era of Oversight,' Tighter Control of FBI Security," *CQ Weekly*, October 5, 2002, p. 2599.

[21] Sen. William S. Cohen, *Roll Call, One Year in the United States Senate* (New York: Simon and Schuster, 1981), p. 293.

[22] Carl Hulse and Robert Pear, "Feeling Left Out on Major Bills, Democrats Turn to Stalling Others," *New York Times*, May 3, 2004, p. A18.

[23] *Congressional Record*, vol. 153, August 3, 2007, p. S10887.

[24] Ibid., September 17, 2007, p. S 11743.

[25] *Congressional Record*, vol. 133, December 9, 1987, p. 34449.

[26] Carroll J. Doherty, "Senate Caught in the Grip Of Its Own 'Holds' System," *Congressional Quarterly Weekly Report*, August 15, 1998, p. 2242.

[27] Ibid.

[28] Brian Friel, "Wrestling With Holds," *National Journal*, January 13, 2007, p. 47.

[29] Stephanie Woodrow, "A Senate Without Secret Holds: How Different?" *Roll Call*, March 30, 2006, p. 46.

[30] Hulse, "Senate May End Its Prized Secrecy In Blocking Bills," p. A13.

[31] See CRS Report RL3 1685, *Proposals to Reform "Holds" in the Senate*, by Walter J. Oleszek.

[32] Hulse, "Senate May End Its Prized Secrecy In Blocking Bills," p. A13.

INDEX